CONTENTS

PREFACE

At some time in the mid-1960s 'participation' became a vogue
word. The accepted wisdom of representative government – the
'rule of the politician' as Schumpeter once called it – came under
pressure from those who wanted a more immediate involvement in
decisions about public policy. It was a time of excitement and
youth: Kennedy was elected President of the United States; a
Labour Government was elected in the United Kingdom; the Bea-
tles introduced an alternative culture; opportunities for higher
education expanded rapidly; and the technological revolution
promised a painless way out of the timeless problems of poverty
and inequality. But for the time being the poor, and especially the
black poor, were still with us. Race riots in America and the muted
echo of unrest in Britain led governments in both countries to
adopt a stance of popular participation in their programmes for
combating poverty. The role of the politician, according to the civil
servant who fathered the British urban programme, was 'to generate consent': public participation would enable this role to be performed more effectively. For a few years no government report was
complete without a section encouraging public participation. The
pressure for a greater measure of public involvement in policy-
making was spreading as the arguments were adopted – and
adapted – by people pursuing a variety of objectives.

The high tide of enthusiasm for public participation is now in
ebb; but attitudes have not settled into their previous pattern. People are less willing than they were to accept authoritarian styles of
leadership. Action groups and public protest have become a regular
feature of policy development. The receding tide leaves pools of
interest where new initiatives are taken, as in recent British government legislation for housing and education. And the arguments are
now beginning about the different purposes that public participa-

tion may serve. Does it promote the interests of those who participate or of those who originate the policies and practices under discussion? From many perspectives the debate about public participation is now conducted at a much deeper level than it was in the
1960s.

For many years we have been concerned with the concept of
public participation as it has affected the policy and provision of
local services in Britain. Most, though not all, of these services are
the responsibility of local government; and those that are not, such
as health and some sections of transportation, have a local government presence in some aspects of the service. Between us we have
conducted research and engaged in teaching in every one of the
fields covered by this book. Our present intention is to review the
impact of public participation in these service fields within the
framework of the broader debate about its purposes. The book is
very much a cooperative endeavour in which each of us has played
a full and equal part: we have, therefore, listed our names in
alphabetical order.

Our conclusions provide lessons both for those optimists who
perceive an increase in public participation as a highway to social
change, and for those pessimists who dismiss it as a cul-de-sac of
co-optation. The structure of our society is powerfully entrenched
and is capable of withstanding or absorbing change from administrative innovation. On the other hand, a greater openness in governmental affairs could provide an opportunity for the general public to join in political debate about the issues involved. So we en-
dorse the experience of public participation in modest tones, with
full appreciation of the counter-arguments that can arise in the
complex development of social conditions.

We are grateful to Iris Walkland for preparing the index to this
book, a culmination of the administrative and editorial assistance
she has provided so conscientiously for us over many years; and
also to our secretarial colleagues who have typed successive drafts.

N.B., M.G., W.A.H., P.S.
January 1981

Chapter One

PARTICIPATION AND LOCAL GOVERNMENT

Quite clearly, the idea of widespread public participation in the process of government is contrary to the idea of representative government on which so much of British central and local government is based. Representative government implies a division of labour in politics in which the ordinary man, *homo civicus*, gives up claims to individual political involvement to the elected representative: the politician, or *homo politicus*, the man for whom politics is a career or an all-consuming passion. In return *homo civicus* expects his elected representative to look after his interests, safe in the knowledge that he will have an opportunity at the ballot box to rid himself of an unsatisfactory *homo politicus* if this should prove necessary – or so the theory would have us believe. The important thing in Britain, of course, is to realise that the process of political socialisation encourages acceptance of the theory as a cultural norm, and discourages the idea that the individual has any right to participate in the process of government. At the national level, and perhaps increasingly at the local level, the theory has been modified to accommodate the idea that organised groups have the right to be consulted by governments on matters that affect them, provided particularly that such groups have demonstrated some kind of ability or willingness to help in the policy-making process, or have convinced those in government that they can help. The right to group consultation is reasonably well established as a cultural norm in British politics, but it is still true to say that widespread public sharing in the process of political decision- and policy-making is not.

This book sets out to detail some of the ways and means by which participation in local government has been encouraged in recent years and to suggest some of the consequences which follow from these changes. Before examining the changes as they relate to specific local services, it is essential to understand some of the main changes in local government and its service provision in recent years. Furthermore the concept of participation as it relates to local government must also be explored.

Whilst a number of attempts have been made to relate the practice of local government to some kind of theoretical framework, it is probably still true to say that in Britain at least there is no theory of local government. There is rather a collection of theories or ideas about the relationship between the individual and his local authority; about the way in which services ought to be provided; and about the division of labour in politics generally, as well as views on the way decisions are taken and policies made in government. Two consequences follow from this: first, what theoretical propositions there are tend to be vague and imprecise, and second, the historical growth of British local government demonstrates a strong *ad hoc*, pragmatic character, reflecting essentially pressures to adapt to short-term difficulties rather than to deal with long-term changes. Put succinctly, the theoretical basis for British local government is vague and its historical development pragmatic.

Looking first at the theoretical underpinnings, two criteria are consistently to be found in the literature (particularly that on reform) from the early nineteenth century onwards. They are first that local government should somehow be democratic (whatever this may mean) and second that it should be efficient (whatever this may mean). As we shall see, it is often held that it is difficult for local government to be *both* democratic and efficient, though not necessarily impossible. For example, *efficient* local government often seems to imply *big* units, so that services can be provided economically and effectively. The efficiency criterion is thus related to service provision, and to the scale of operation necessary to provide the services. In essence, the efficiency criterion is supported by those who believe big means better, and it is those concerned about such services as planning, transportation, education, housing and health who have most frequently argued the case for larger units of local government, advocating such changes on efficiency grounds.

By contrast the case for democratic local government is more difficult to put succinctly, but it has strong emotional and normative overtones. Indeed, these are so strong that even those who argue for big, efficient local government are likely to advocate that such a system should be democratic. Ideas about democratic local government range from the classical Greek city state in which all citizens participated equally in the process of their government through the ideas of representative government at the local level associated with John Stuart Mill through to present-day formulations, such as modern pluralism, in which local politics is seen as a process of bargaining among a collection of differing but not necessarily equal groups. In each of these formulations, three themes can be distinguished, one perhaps more recent than the other two.

First, the idea of locality or of community is inherently bound up with ideas about democracy. Democratic government is local government: democratic government is community government. It is as if it were people's sense of place and locality, their identification with a particular area, community or neighbourhood, which somehow imparts to them a feeling of involvement or a sense of democracy. This leads almost inevitably to the second theme, namely that democratic government is only possible in small-scale communities or rural areas, and that somehow once areas grow to the size of the present-day town or city the task of governing them democratically becomes enormously difficult if not impossible. Indeed it was to meet the changes posed by the rapid industrialisation and urbanisation of late eighteenth- and early nineteenth-century England that Mill developed his ideas about representative government, with the implication that as the scale of government increased, the involvement of the individual in local government inevitably has to be limited and more indirect.

The third theme underlying democratic local government is that such government is open and accessible to the individual or group. That is to say, those who wish to take part in the decision- and policy-making processes can do so fairly easily and they can have an influence over the decisions taken locally which affect them, should they so wish. Much of British government, at both central and local levels, is characterised by its closed, secretive nature, and by the difficulties people face in dealing with governmental institutions. For example, people often experience difficulties in learning about planning and development proposals in a particular area or establishing their rights to welfare benefits. Often people and groups feel unable to influence such proposals and issues, and advocates of open, accessible local government might point to such examples to suggest that the present welfare system is somewhat undemocratic.

All these theories and ideas about democratic local government represent normative ideals rarely if ever attained in practice, even in the best of New England town meetings. The Greeks excluded slaves from the process of government; the Swiss excluded women from canton government; and the government of rural England was (and in some parts perhaps still is) the province of the aristocracy and local squirearchy. Certainly widespread mass participation in local affairs has not been a common English phenomenon, though support for the idea that local government ought to be democratic is widespread.

At the centre of the conflict between the two criteria of democracy and efficiency in local government lies the important question of the most appropriate *scale* of operation and organisation of local government. For those who believe in participant democracy, 'small is beautiful', whilst for those who want efficient local government 'big is better'! The constant pull between these two criteria is what affects the scale of local government, and in this century at least the pull of efficiency has been the stronger, resulting in a larger scale of local government in Britain than might have otherwise been the case.

Thus from the mid-nineteenth century onwards the scale of British local government's organisation and operations has constantly increased. The last hundred years has seen a massive change from private provision of services to public provision: a move from private government to public government. The modern resident of metropolitan Birmingham can no longer hope for anything like the self-sufficiency the rural resident of one hundred years ago might have expected or claimed. He now expects his local authority to house, educate and transport him, as well as supporting him in ways which would have been unthinkable one hundred years ago. And it is the process of industrialisation and urbanisation which has created a rather different kind of interdependence from that which existed in preindustrial times. This process of industrialisation and the accompanying growth of towns and cities brought with it a division of labour which has resulted in a high level of individual and areal specialisation in urban areas. Not only are people individually very highly specialised, but even areas of our towns and cities are very specialised, so that the business area has become separated from the industrial, and these in turn are separated from the residential areas. The consequent demand for transportation between these different areas gives rise to one of the more difficult problems facing modern metropolitan governments, that of congestion.

The growth and change in local government that have taken place in the face of these social and economic changes give rise to a number of common themes, four of which are of concern to us here. The changes themselves will be examined in more detail in the next chapter, and our task here is to explore the themes and then to discuss the concept of participation as it relates to them.

The four features or themes can be summarised as functional fragmentation; centralisation of government; professionalisation of service provision; and the increasing remoteness of government from people. Though treated here separately, the four themes are closely interrelated, as the subsequent discussion will show.

First, the question of functional fragmentation. Most of the changes which have taken place in British local government have been functional ones rather than areal ones. Essentially the boundaries and structure of local authorities remained largely intact from the late nineteenth-century reforms until the recent reorganisation in 1974, with the notable exception of London and a few county borough changes. By contrast, the services provided by local authorities increased tremendously: functions such as housing, planning, public transport, full-scale education, and so on are mainly twentieth-century functions. Even though local government has lost some functions, such as gas and electricity supply, health and water services to other *ad hoc* agencies, the balance has really been on the side of local government in terms of increased service provision. Furthermore, most of these services have simply been added to those already provided by local authorities, with, until the last ten years, very little concern for co-ordination or for the establishment of priorities between services. As each new service arrived, local authorities simply created a new department to administer it and established yet another council committee to oversee it. Perhaps one of the best examples is education, where as the service grew, particularly after the 1944 Education Act, so did the size, scope and power of the education department in those local authorities responsible for providing education. In some cases, education powers were fully delegated by councils to their education committees, who in turn reported to council on an information only basis, so that education policy was rarely if ever discussed in the full council. At the same time, with the spread of council housing, accelerated with the introduction of widescale slum clearance programmes in the mid 1950s, large housing departments were established in our main urban authorities, but often operating with little co-ordination or co-operation with education or social service departments, two other departments most likely to be involved with housing. It was thus not unusual for a housing department to evict tenants for rent arrears and then to be asked to find accommodation for the same people by the social services department dealing with them as a homeless family. If the family had school age children, the education department could also be involved with the family, dealing with truancy problems. The family could find itself dealing with three or more local authority departments whose own co-operation was minimal.

It is this kind of fragmentation of function, of local service provision, which gave rise to criticism of the managerial capacity and policy-making structure of local authorities in the late 1960s and early 1970s and which provided the main impetus behind the corporate planning movement then fashionable in local government circles. And whilst it is possible to exaggerate the extent to which service provision was fragmented before the 1974 reorganisation, it still remains true that such functional fragmentation remains a characteristic of many local authorities in the post-reorganisation period. Whilst the majority of local authorities have adopted some variation of corporate planning, there are many cases and instances where aspects of the old separation still prevails. Education departments, for example, have claimed that it is difficult and/or unnecessary for them to become part of the corporate planning system, complaining bitterly when some 'outsider' from the corporate planning unit questions their intentions and proposals.

The second theme to be explored here concerns the centralisation of government in twentieth-century Britain and its impact on local government. Space forbids a detailed discussion of the ways in which the process of government has increasingly centred on Whitehall and Parliament. In part this centralisation follows from the ever increasing scope of government business itself, expanding as it has in response both to people's demands for bigger and better services, and to the greatly increased problems of economic management which have followed changes in Britain's economic position in the world. But these changes in government activity only explain part of the centralisation process, much of which has been due to the fact that central government, or rather the two major political parties, have been increasingly concerned with the problems of equalisation and redistribution of resources among different people, groups, classes and areas. In other words, much of twentieth-century British government has been about correcting the balance between rich and poor, be the problem seen in terms of people or areas. And in general terms, the task of equalising or redistributing resources and services has been seen as one which can only really be achieved by central government. Only the centre, it is argued, is concerned with the national overall interest: by contrast local governments are more self-interested, and concerned with maintaining differentials.

This centralisation process has had a number of consequences for local government in Britain. First, it should be noted that central government has rarely itself been the means by which equalisation and redistribution have been achieved, with the possible exception of social security (DHSS) and regional policies (Department of Trade and Industry). In many services, such as education, housing, police, central government has increased the range and scope of service provision, but required *local* authorities to provide the actual services on the ground, whilst developing large central departments, such as the Department of the Environment, to oversee the local authorities in the hope that the latter will provide the services to the required minimum level. It is worth noting in passing that central government's ability to persuade local authorities to do something which they do not wish to do has been remarkably low, as some of the attempts at introducing comprehensive education in areas like Tameside, West Yorkshire and Surrey indicate.

Second, as central government has increased the number and range of services provided by local authorities, so has its share of the financial burden, with central government grants now accounting for almost two-thirds of local government's current expenditure. At the same time, the amount of local authority income derived from local property taxes, that is the rates, has declined continuously throughout the century. This increasing central contribution to the cost of local service provision has given rise to important questions of control, discretion and accountability, as the (Layfield) Committee of Inquiry into Local Government Finance well demonstrated. Given the confusion as to who actually determines the level of service provision in many areas of government activity, central or local, how is it possible to enforce ideas about accountability and responsibility? Should not locally determined services be financed by local sources of income and nationally determined ones financed from national sources? The important point for our purposes is that the present confused situation in terms of both finance and service levels makes it difficult to see to what extent local government really has sufficient discretion and autonomy for it to be described as local government. In practice, the confusion may be to the advantage of both central departments and local authorities, in that there is enough slack in the system of central–local relations for each side to justify its actions. But given that this confused situation is part of the centralisation process, it clearly has implications for the way in which local government works, which in turn will relate to the question of public participation.

So far, we have been looking at the centralisation process essentially from the central perspective, but there is a sense in which local government itself has contributed to the process. This is through what Young (1975) has aptly called 'the delocalisation of local politics'. Three features of this delocalisation process may be briefly mentioned. First there is the change in the type of person running local authorities, particularly in terms of elected members. This is a change summarised by Lee (1963) as one from a style of leadership based on social leaders, whose social and economic status was not dependent in any way on their political activity, to one where the leaders are public persons, whose social status is very much dependent on political activity. There have been changes even since Lee wrote his book, so that it would be more accurate to say that the public persons are now very much *party* ones, owing this position to their party activity and ties. Indeed, the rise of national parties at the local level is the second feature of the delocalisation process to be noted. Whilst politics could be found in local government in the nineteenth century, particularly in the main urban areas, the spread of party politics into local government is very much a twentienth-century occurrence, in that it is during the last fifty years that the national parties have organised themselves not only to fight local elections but also to adopt party policy platforms, to seek positions of power in the council and to adopt the ideas of the precouncil caucus meeting and the imposition of the party whip as a way of ensuring that they control the policies adopted by the council. Indeed, local government now provides many examples of one party states, where the council is heavily dominated by either the Labour or Conservative party, whilst the twentieth century has also seen the decline of the old fashioned independent non-partisan councillor.

The third feature of the delocalisation process is the rise of the national associations of local authorities and the ever increasing role they play *vis-à-vis* central government. For example, the associations play an important part in the annual negotiations to determine the level of the rate support grant, and were described as long ago as 1956 as 'part of the constitution' by the then Minister of Housing and Local Government, Duncan Sandys. Indeed it would be impossible to think of any piece of central government business which affects local authorities on which these associations are not consulted. But these are national associations, concerned with all the authorities of a particular type – county or shire district for example – rather than with individual authorities, and their increased involvement is likely to mean reduced contact between individual authorities and the centre.

The professionalisation and bureaucratisation of local government comprise another theme we wish to explore. Whilst there have always been some professions in local government, notably the nineteenth-century engineers and medical officers of health, this century has seen the introduction of a number of new specialist professionals into local government. Thus town planners, social workers, environmental health officers, educationalists, have all appeared since 1900. Within the last twenty years, newer professional groups have emerged, such as housing managers, recreation/ leisure managers, policy analysts and corporate planners. Each has claimed his own expertise and specialist right to dominate some service arena to the exclusion of other local government officers. The various specialists have their own professional standards and seek to control the numbers and quality of new entrants into the profession, as well as expressing views nationally about the standards of the service for which they are responsible. Town planning provides an excellent example of this professionalism. The associations hold annual meetings at which members can exchange views or learn of new developments. One consequence is that individual professional officers develop a dual loyalty, one to the authority which employs him (an areal loyalty) and one to the national association (a professional loyalty), and it is often difficult to say which is the more important. A further consequence is that standards of service provision thought appropriate to local government may come to be determined by national associations rather than by the actual needs of a particular authority.

One reason for the emergence of specialist professions in local government also accounts in part for its bureaucratic nature, namely that much of what local government does has become extremely complex in nature and often requires considerable technical expertise to understand. For example, attempting to understand the complexity of inner city deprivation requires an understanding of the social, economic and political processes which have led to that deprivation.

To deal with this complexity, local authorities, like all large-scale organisations, have developed bureaucratic styles of decision- and policy-making. We take bureaucratic to mean that the process of work within any local authority department is organised in a hierarchical fashion, with different levels of responsibility, clearly demarcated areas of work, established lines of communication between different levels of the hierarchy, and well-defined information flows. Thus, to illustrate this point, whilst a departmental chief officer is theoretically responsible for all the work done in the department, much of the work leading to the policy advice will be done by staff working at three or four levels removed from the chief. These staff may never get to attend the relevant committee or council meeting where their advice is presented. Very often items may be presented to committee about which the chief officer, or his deputy, may in practice know very little, the assumption being that the work has been done properly at the appropriate level in the bureaucracy.

The spread of professionalism and the bureaucratisation of local government have had important consequences for the elected member, who is essentially the unpaid amateur politician, formally responsible for an authority's policies and provision of services. At best it is difficult for this amateur to meet the professional expert on anything like equal terms: length of service, knowledge of a particular area, time spent as a committee chairman or deputy, or some recognised political standing or professional competence are what makes it possible for the elected member to cope with his professional officers. But at worst it is impossible for a councillor to face officers on anything like equal terms, particularly where they are inexperienced or are unable to grasp the complexity of much council business. In such a situation, councillors probably have little choice but to accept their officers' advice. Yet without wishing to restate the false distinction between policy and administration or to deny that officials do not take part in the political decisions of their local authority, it is important to remember that in both the public eye and in terms of the theory of representative government, it is the elected member who is supposedly responsible and accountable for those policy decisions. Indeed, it may well be that because people no longer necessarily think councillors are really the effective policy-makers, but that it is the officials – the unknown bureaucrats – who run things, that there is so much apparent disillusionment with or lack of interest in local government among the mass of people today.

This links in with the fourth theme we want to discuss, namely

that local government has become remote from the people it seeks
to serve. The previous three themes, fragmentation of services, centralisation of government, the professionalisation and bureaucratisation of local government have all contributed to the idea that local
government has become remote from its residents. Indeed, we would
argue that local government reorganisation, with larger authorities,
bigger departments and fewer elected members, has contributed
to this remoteness, and that the establishment of two-tier government in the main metropolitan areas has worsened the situation.
How, for example, do the people of Hyde or Stalybridge identify
with the new Tameside, of which few people outside of Greater
Manchester will have heard until its celebrated victory over the
Secretary of State over comprehensive education? The people of
Leigh and Tyldesley live in those towns and not in some strange
unknown planet called Wigan, even if that is where they pay their
rates, complain about services or seek planning permission. Councillors have to deal with 6,000 or 7,000 constituents or more and
not the 2,000 to 3,000 they might have had before reorganisation.
In some authorities, residents have to travel considerable distances
to visit a particular department or go to the town hall. In all these
ways, local government has become more distant, more remote,
with public and their officials and councillors becoming increasingly
divorced from each other. As we shall see, attempts at area management, community councils, divisional organisation, delegation
and agency are all efforts designed to bridge the gap, as is the use
of council-produced newspapers. But the channels between the individual and his elected representative have become increasingly
blocked, less effective, so that the former seeks to deal either
directly with the officials responsible for dealing with his problem
or to work with others in some kind of organised group. And it
might well be argued that when people become divorced from and
disinterested in the work of their local authority that local government ceases to be *local* government and becomes simply a branch
or adjunct of government generally.

How does the idea of participation fit into this picture of local
government and how does it relate to our four themes particularly?
It would be wrong to suggest that participation is a panacea for all
the problems facing British local government, though there is
sometimes a tendency for the advocates of participation to act as if
this were true. Participation is a chimeric word, capable of meaning many things to many people. Indeed, even *The Shorter Oxford
English Dictionary* gives at least two definitions: one implies the

idea of forming part of something, the second that of sharing something in common with others, or taking part with others, in some action or other. Essentially, when we are talking of public participation in local government we are using the word in this latter sense, that is to say, we imply that people are taking part, with others, in their local government. But, as we shall see, even this idea is capable of many different interpretations and meanings. For example, at one extreme, we might say that participation is about power and that public participation in local government is about shifting the balance of power away from those in formal positions of authority in local government (members and officials) towards individual people or groups in the locality or community. At another extreme, participation might be considered as the right of people to make representations, to express one's views, or to be given a hearing on matters which affect them, without any corollary that such representations will be taken into account by those responsible for running local government, let alone that such representations would affect the decisions to be made. Alternatively, participation may mean that only certain groups or individuals may be given opportunities to share in the running of local government, either because those in power consider this fit and proper or else because they feel such people are of such importance that their views ought to be taken into account in the decision- and policy-making processes. As we said at the outset, ideas such as these run counter to that of representative government, which is at the heart of both central and local government in Britain.

There is another sense in which the term public participation is used, and that is in the way it is linked to ideas about open, accessible government. Three themes are involved in this concept. First there is the idea of exchanging information between government and public – of a two-way flow of information between both sides. Involved here are ideas of publicising governmental proposals, of telling people what a local authority is doing or might do, and generally making such information widely available: this is essentially the *publicity* of government. Equally, this involves the idea of people transmitting information back to government, for example, of local authorities seeking information from the public on a variety of issues. Information collection of this sort might very well form part of participation.

Second, open, accessible government involves the idea of open decisions, openly arrived at. In local government terms this would mean committee and council meetings (and indeed perhaps party caucus meetings) open to press and public alike. Then, say advocates of this view, at least people will know that councillors and officials – the local authority – have nothing to hide. Like the first theme, this view of open, accessible government assures a largely passive role for the public, especially those who might be persuaded that attending a council or committee meeting is a better pastime than watching TV or walking the dog.

The third sense of open accessible government suggests improving and perhaps increasing the channels of communication between the local authority and its public. It involves making it easier for elected representatives, officials, individuals and groups to establish contact with each other and exchange information, views and ideas. Making government more accessible does not necessarily mean greater participation: it only means increasing the opportunities for participation, and people may or may not choose to take them up.

Each of these views of participation reflects different values or beliefs. Much of this book will be concerned with examining how different perspectives on participation have affected the various attempts made to increase public participation in the provision of a number of services. Thus planners, educationalists, social workers and others are all likely to adopt different ideological positions about participation, which in turn will affect the way public participation happens in relation to particular services. Similarly participation is likely to vary with the level or agency of government responsible for the particular service: some of the service areas dealt with later, such as health, and trunk road and motorway planning, are the responsibility of central government or an *ad hoc* agency. Both are likely to bring a different perspective to participation from those whose main area of service provision is in local government. Encouraging participation in service provision is not simply a question of adopting the same techniques and engaging some homogeneous public: the services vary, and so do the public. We have drawn a distinction in the book between participation in physical services, such as planning and housing, participation in personal services, such as health and social services, and participation which is areally defined. Each produces its own forms of participation, with different results for the different service areas.

In part this reflects the different participatory mechanisms which have been adopted in relation to the various services. In some cases, conflict appears to have arisen between the 'new fangled' public participation and local authority, as some of the Com-

Public participation in local services

munity Development Project experience shows, though whether all
that has happened is that latent conflict has been made explicit is
another question. In other cases official and elected members may
feel, correctly or incorrectly, that their role in the policy-making
process has been threatened: this has perhaps been the experience
in the planning field. In other services, such as transport, much of
the participation encouraged by government has been of a somewhat token kind, in which participation has largely been concerned
with giving and collecting information, though in other cases, such
as motorway enquiries, members of the public have used the
opportunity to challenge the whole basis of the road planning procedure.

Nevertheless, so far we have been talking about participation as
if it is something novel, when in fact most people become involved
with their local government in some way or other. People pay rates,
vote in local elections, write to newspapers on particular issues,
join political parties, or voluntary groups, or else they contact
councillors or officials on some matter. Indeed, it might be argued
that people participate simply as users of services, and social and
health services provide interesting examples where user participation is a particularly important category. Despite this, surveys repeatedly suggest that the numbers participating on any issue are
generally low, and that those who participate tend to be overwhelmingly, but not exclusively, middle class, better educated, long-
term residents well established in their community. In other words,
participation in local affairs depends not only upon the opportunities, but also on the skills and motivation which people have for
participation. Undoubtedly there are variations in people's willingness and ability to become involved in political discussion.

In the first place, there has to be some basis or focus for participation. This may be provided at an areal level, where it is identification with a particular locality which encourages people to become involved, as with residents' associations or community
groups; or it may be in terms of some shared interest or activity,
such as happens with music lovers, good food enthusiasts or football
fans. Or, as is the focus of this book particularly, the basis for
participation may be functional or service orientated, as it is with
groups and individuals concerned with housing and welfare services. In each of these cases there is something sufficient at least to
form a point from which individual or group participation can
develop.

But motivation has also to be stronger than the sharing of or

14

identification with a particular cause. Individuals or groups have to feel strongly about something if they are to take action about it. The issue has to matter to them, particularly if they are to become involved on a sustained basis over time. Having a stake in something or feeling passionate about an issue is what moves people to participate. But what triggers this motivation is difficult to discern: it may be something small or large, such as threatened demolition or failure to empty the bins.

Once stirred, people have to use their participatory skills, or else develop them if they are to participate. Skill covers a variety of possibilities from knowing someone who can 'fix it' to writing letters; from organising petitions and protest meetings to diplomatically persuading councillors, officials, even Ministers and civil servants that one's case is valid, just or right. Some people have these skills inherently, perhaps because of their education or occupation, or because they have lived in an area for a long time and know what participatory channels are available to them. Others have limited or undeveloped skills, which can only be improved or widened by the experience of participation or through encouragement by others. Suffice it to say here that people need not only a focus and motivation, but also some skill if they are to participate. Even so, there will be degrees of individual and group participation. People will vary in their activism, from their relatively passive participation as service users in most cases, to their participation in the provision of services, as with voluntary groups in some social services, until they are actively concerned with persuading and deciding what policies for service provision will be. Participation can be direct, as when people actively confront their local authority on policy issues, or it can be indirect, as when they offer support to a campaigning group, leaving others to direct operations.

Enough has been said here to show that participation, far from being a simple concept, is indeed a complex one. Participation means many things to many people, but there is a need to summarise and to simplify for our purposes. Many of the recent moves to encourage public participation *vis à vis* a number of public services have come from the side of the governors, as elected members and professional officers have sought to bring about some kind of public participation in the provision of the services for which they are responsible. These moves towards participation can be seen as *a* counter, but not *the* counter, to some of the problems created by the services fragmentation, the centralisation of government, the professionalisation and bureaucratisation of services, and the general remoteness of government. Many of the opportunities for participation, and the techniques and mechanisms used, have been devised by those who provide the services – by the governors themselves, and as such this participatory framework has very much been determined by the constraints under which officials and elected representatives have operated and by the ideological perspective they bring to participation itself.

It is points like these which underlie the viewpoint of those, often Marxist, writers who see participation of this type as a means of manipulating the public into acceptance of bureaucratically determined policy solutions, of the *status quo*, or of 'the necessity' of the capitalist system. In this sense public participation is seen as undermining or subverting the 'genuine' interest of (particularly working class) individuals and groups.

But there has also been a movement towards participation from below, from the ranks of the governed, as individuals and groups of people have sought to become involved in the process of governing themselves. Tenants threatened by rent increases; residents by demolition; environmentalists by pollution, or those simply wanting to do something which involves a public service, all have joined the movement towards participation. In most, if not nearly all cases, this participation has involved conflict, as governors and governed clash over policy and service provision matters. In other cases, appeals to participate by officials and representatives have reached only deaf ears. In still others, demands for participation by people have met a wall of silence. Sometimes, perhaps more frequently than we are often led to suspect, people, officials and members – the governors and the governed – meet on equal terms; their ideologies overlap, and they can agree on the nature and purpose of participation. Conflicts still occur, but their resolution may be easier, for the rules of the participation game are agreed. In these cases, the participation process is itself beneficial, for those involved learn from it; they become educated in the art of politics, and in Mill's terms, they become better citizens. At a normative level, perhaps this is the end which participation serves, for participation is not an end in itself, but a means to an end. But this is a theme to which we shall return later in the book: for now, we must turn to a consideration of the recent developments in local government which have led to the situation in which the present debate takes place.

Chapter two
THE INSTITUTIONAL CONTEXT OF PUBLIC PARTICIPATION

In the last chapter we identified four trends in recent British local government which had increased demands for public participation in the provision of local public services. They were the increasing fragmentation of services and functions at local level; the increasing centralisation of British government and the complexity this has brought to central–local relations; the increased involvement of professional officials in the provision of local services; and last, the increasing remoteness, or divorce, of governments, both local and central, from the people they exist to serve. This chapter examines these trends more fully, concentrating particularly on the period after 1945, since it is in this post-Second World War era that the growing complexity of life in general and of public service provision by governments in particular has become specifically a crucial problem, not just in Britain but in most Western societies. Today, critics of both the Left and the Right question the ability of governments to cope with service crises and raise issues of the legitimacy and acceptability of much of government action as we move into the post-industrial society.

In essence, the issues involved have to be resolved at two levels. First, at the *local* level, since this is where most of us act out our lives, notwithstanding the marked tendency people have to work in one place and live in another. Most of us identify with something less than the national community: we are Lancastrians or Men of Kent; residents of Sheffield or Liverpool; part of the town or village community, rather than part of the wider society. In other words, our focus is on the *local* community. The same is true of the way in which we consume our public goods and services: most of us send children to *local*, or neighbourhood, schools, we rent our house from a *local* authority, not a national one, just as we borrow books at the local library; visit a district hospital and have refuse collected locally. The point essentially is that both the production and the consumption of public goods and services are undertaken at the local level rather than at the national level: it is local governments and agencies who deliver the services, not national government, by and large.

Second, however, the issues also have to be resolved (and increasingly are) at the *national* level. As we saw in the previous chapter, all four themes have contributed to the nationalisation of British politics: moving issues off the local on to the national scene. Despite pressures for devolution and decentralisation in the late 1960s and early 1970s, British governmental and political processes have increasingly focused on Whitehall and Westminster, and despite the considerable territorial and areal variations which exist in the provision of public services in Britain, there has been an increasing tendency for the debate on these services to take place at the national level among an increasingly *national* community of actors drawn from the ranks of Ministers and politicians, from central government officials; from *national* associations of local authorities and professional officials, together with people from the statutory undertakers, nationalised industries and other quasi-governmental agencies. In essence, the policy debate about public goods and services is conducted at the *national* level by a *national* community, yet the same goods and services are, by and large, produced, delivered and consumed by *local* people at the *local* level. Thus, for example, the debates over the 1980 Education and Housing Acts, which involved such issues as the price of school meals and school transport as well as the sale of council houses and tenant involvement in council house management, were conducted essentially at national level, even though the detailed policy decisions are made by local education and housing authorities. At the centre of much of the current debate is the issue of finance, particularly the level of public expenditure generally and the central contribution to local government expenditure particularly. For example, most of the opposition to the 1980 Local Government Act centred around the new block grant and the powers central government has to penalise what it sees as overspending authorities. Again this issue was played out on the *national* stage by the *national* associations of local government. The overall result of this centralisation process is that the national debate constrains local debate and may result in limits being placed on local discretion.

Public participation has been part of the national debate, as our discussion of such policy arenas as planning and social services will show. The problem is that one suspects that the motives and interests of those involved in the *national* debate are rather different from those concerned or involved in the locality. Resolving the national debate frequently means leaving issues still to be resolved locally, perhaps even complicating their successful resolution: again, the statutory introduction of public participation into planning provides an example. That the policy debate takes place at a national level is a reflection of the first two trends mentioned earlier: functional specialisation and governmental centralisation, reinforced by the third, namely increased professionalisation of service provision. How has this occurred? Functional specialisation in terms of service provision reflects first the way in which individual services have emerged on a separate basis – education, health, housing and transport – and second the increase in demands and expectations which we have about public services generally and which largely reflect changes in living standards, particularly since 1945. Life in Britain, despite the current economic crisis and rising unemployment, is very different from what it was thirty-five years ago. The spread of television (especially colour TV); the increase in car ownership and of other consumer durables; increased owner occupation, whereby over half the population own or are buying their houses; longer and more frequent holidays both at home and abroad, have all changed people's perceptions of what life is about and what constitutes 'the good life', however materialistic such a view may be. And just as this increased standard of living has meant an increase in the consumption of privately produced goods, so has it meant an increase in the expectations and consumption people have of public goods and services. Thus, we want bigger, better schools with lower teacher/pupil ratios; we want more leisure centres/recreation areas opened up by public authorities, and better roads/public transport to deliver us to them.

Until the early/mid-1970s, the increased consumption of both private and public goods could be financed out of continuing economic growth, however limited it might be, so that yesterday's luxuries quickly became tomorrow's necessities. The response of government at the centre to these rising demands and rising expectations was to meet them by increasing public sector provision, financed during the periods when the economy was in a 'go' or growth condition, cut back when it was in a 'stop' or decline situation. But generally continuing economic growth in Britain allowed the centre to introduce and develop an increasing number of new services (for example in the personal social services and leisure areas) as well as undertaking a restructuring and reorganisation of existing ones (for example, education, health and water), together with a massive reorganisation of the structure of British local government. Since the mid-1970s, of course, the economic and financial situations have been such that cuts in public goods and services have been the order of the day: imposed by central government but felt most heavily in the locality. Service standards have suffered also from the high rates of inflation the country has experienced since the early 1970s, a situation further aggravated by the central imposition of cash limits on supplementary grants which fail to meet the full effects of inflation.

The centre's concern for these kinds of issues stems from a number of sources. First, government at the centre assumes a responsibility for the national interest. In service terms, government departments concerned with overseeing the services for which they are responsible will attempt to ensure that these services reach certain minimum standards across the country as a whole, particularly where the services are a statutory obligation upon local authorities and other governmental agencies. The 1976 drought provides an illustration of the point, in that when it became apparent that severe water shortages threatened parts of the country, it was the centre which intervened to see that water resources were moved around. For example, there was even talk of moving water out of Scotland into England by tanker, a suggestion strongly opposed by localist orientated Scottish Nationalists. There was discussion about the possible construction of a national water grid, the large cost of which could only be met out of central government funds. By contrast, local governments are concerned with the needs for services in their particular locality: if needs are high, then an authority might provide a service above the national minimum standard, whereas if they are low, the temptation to fall below that standard or not to provide a service at all, will be very great. If the centre is concerned about uniformity and minimum standards, by contrast the local authority is concerned with differences and special interests, namely those pertaining to it.

Second, however, the centre is also concerned with service provision because of its overarching concern with issues of economic management, with efficiency and with the increasing central contribution to the financing of services. Not only is this latter point particularly relevant in relation to local government, as the arguments over the Government's 1980 Local Government and Planning Act illustrate, but also the centre has had to meet the increasing cost of such other services as health care and social security benefits.

Whilst it is commonplace to stress the growing complexity and interdependence of national and world economies, one of the major developments in British politics since 1945 remains the increased part played in the economy by central government, not only in terms of its budgetary and taxation policies, but also because of its concern about such issues as wages and prices, for regional economic variations, and concern for both state and private manufacturing activities such as British Steel and Ferranti. Until the election in 1979 of Mrs Thatcher and her monetarist-inclined Conservative Government, the post-war period was largely dominated by a consensus on economic policy based on Keynesian ideas of economic management. Part of this consensus involved consideration of the part played by the public sector in the economy generally and by local government in particular. The need for economic management at the national level (in all its various guises) also included the need to control public sector activity generally, and that of local government in particular, since it was the fastest growing element in the public sector. If central government's economic policies were to have a chance of working, then control would have to be exercised over the activities of local government: it would have to conform with the *national* priorities set by the centre.

The election of the Conservatives in May 1979 added a further dimension to the arguments about economic management, for it brought a government with a different set of economic theories (monetarist as distinct to Keynesian) and also more committed to reducing the size and scope of the public sector than any government since 1945. This brought the centre into sharp conflict with the national organs of local government in particular, especially over the financial provisions of the new Act, but also over its legislation in the housing and education fields.

The financial element in the central–local relationship and the attempts by the centre to restrict the total of local expenditures largely reflect the arguments about economic management, but are also a reflection of the centre's concern with efficiency in service provision, where efficiency by and large means providing services at the lowest possible financial cost, though the centre also has a concern with services from a perspective which stresses ideas of equity and parity. Local government has increasingly been dependent upon the centre for the finance it needs to provide its various services: so much so that around 60 per cent of current reckonable expenditure is met from central government grants (particularly from the general Rate Support Grant, RSG), whilst capital expenditure is mainly financed from the government backed Public Works Loans Board and prior central government approval has to be sought. This control over loan sanction, as it is called, means that the centre has had greater control over local government *capital* expenditure than over *current* expenditure, but perhaps less than some would like.

The issue of local government finance is a complicated one, beyond the scope of this book. But it is important to realise the control implications for the centre of its massive financial support for local government: whilst there is some evidence, e.g. Layfield, that the financiers of the piper have not always wanted to call the tune, there must be little doubt that local authorities believe the centre could do so if it wished, as the heated debate over the proposed switch to a block grant system of finance suggested (Layfield 1976; SOLACE/INLOGOV 1980).

A third reason for the increasing involvement of the centre also reflects the interdependent nature of many of the problems and issues with which governments, both central and local, have to deal. This increasing interdependence raises critical questions about the appropriate level of state action to deal with the issues and indeed it may raise doubts about the capacity of government, at whatever level, to cope with the problems. Doubts about the ability of *local* government to provide the kinds of services expected of it certainly underlay the reform proposals of the late 1960s and early 1970s, culminating in the reorganisation associated with the 1972 Local Government Act. Similar issues and doubts were involved in the organisation of the health service and the water authorities: the late 1960s/early 1970s were very much caught up in the mood/ search for managerial and service efficiency, a reflection perhaps of the belief that technological change would be universally beneficial. 'Bigger means better' would capture the mood of the times, both in the public and private sectors, for the latter saw its own structural transformation during the period through the process of mergers and takeovers and the development of multinational corporations.

The reorganisation of local government in the early 1970s provides an example of this concern with governmental efficiency. Established in 1888, the old system had remained largely intact on an areal basis but with an ever changing functional one right up until the early 1970s. By the mid-1960s most commentators within and without local government considered the system inadequate, and the then Minister of Housing and Local Government, Richard Crossman, established a Royal Commission under the chairmanship of Sir John (later Lord Redcliffe) Maud in 1966. Reporting three years later, the Commission stressed such weaknesses in the system as the meaningless conflict between town and country, the inefficient division of functions between the counties and their districts and the fact that the small size of many authorities meant they were unable to provide a full range of services efficiently. But the Commission also underlined weaknesses in the democratic nature of the system: many people were both ignorant of, and lacked interest in, what the local authorities do, and furthermore the authorities were, in the Commission's eyes, little more than the agents of the domineering centre. In this the Commission were simply reiterating what has been called the conventional wisdom about central-local relations.

In suggesting a new structure designed to overcome these weaknesses, the Commission went for a simplified, hopefully more efficient, system better able to stand up to a strong centre. In proposing single tier unitary authorities for most of the country, however, the Commission were advocating efficiency at the expense of the more democratic criteria, quickly arousing the criticism that their proposals would make local government even more remote from the people it was designed to serve.

Whilst the largely urban-based proposals were acceptable to the then Labour Government, the Conservative Government elected in June 1970 rejected them, accepting many of the criticisms made by the Commission's opponents. Yet in providing its own two-tier system, based on the rural, shire counties and the experience of the GLC, the Conservatives failed to strengthen the system in either democratic or efficiency terms, but in effect fell between the two competing sets of criteria. The resultant local government system as we know it today is thus neither as efficient nor as democratic (i.e. close to the people) as it might otherwise have been. Yet it remains one of the 1970s' monuments to the goal of efficiency, equalled in the public sector probably only by the reform of the health service and water authorities and by the predilection for massive units of production on the part of the British Steel Corporation.

If the search for efficiency in service delivery and concern for economic management were two pressures operating since 1945 which encouraged the centralisation of British politics, then the activity of organised groups seeking to extend public goods and services was a third. It was also, we suspect, the major force behind the ever increasing fragmentation and specialisation of these services. As most recent books on interest groups note, it is unusual for central government to initiate new policy or produce major shifts in existing policy without having consulted those groups it recognises as having a special interest in the policy under review. Indeed in the late 1970s, this sort of development led some writers to write of corporatism and the corporate state, talking about partnership between government and the major interests concerned. In part this reflected the kind of development under the 1974–79 Labour Government with its development of incomes policy in discussion particularly with the TUC (the social wage) and also the CBI, but it could be argued that this development was paralleled in other policy areas. The worlds of local government and the welfare services, including housing, provide good examples. The restructuring of the personal social services, following the publication of the Seebohm Committee Report in 1968, is a case in point. Its recommendations reflected three issues, each of which was of concern to particular organised interests. First, there was the pressure for a unified social service department to be created inside local authorities, a move advocated by an élite group of social policy experts, and social administration practitioners, foremost among whom was Richard Titmuss. Second, there was pressure concerning the role of the voluntary sector in the future of social services delivery, with Seebohm advocating a stronger part in both the planning and provision of these services. Voluntary groups of all kinds have always been very heavily involved in social service provision, despite the increased role of both the national and local state in welfare service provision in the twentieth century. This policy sector is one in which participation in public policy-making and service provision is most highly developed, involving as it does a range from such well-known national groups as the NSPCC, Age Concern, the WRVS and the Child Poverty Action Group right down to locally based charities and service organisations.

The third issue, also related to one of our themes, concerned the growing professionalisation of social work generally and within local authority social services departments as well. It was particularly relevant in the late 1960s and early 1970s, a period during which there were still many unqualified social workers employed by local authorities and when the range and type of social work was increasing. Since the reorganisation of the personal social service departments in the early 1970s, there have been further developments in social services, particularly in terms of services for the physically and mentally handicapped, as well as for the elderly and homeless, and despite the creation of unified social service departments, there still remains a tendency to specialisation among social workers, rather than the full blown development of a generic variety, the activities of the British Association of Social Workers notwithstanding.

The specialisation of services is also a reflection of the third theme, namely the increased role of the paid official in the policy-making process. In shorthand terms, this is usually described as the increased professionalisation and bureaucratisation of local government and involves the idea that policies and service levels are increasingly determined by the expert, technically competent, paid officials working in local government.

Whilst there have always been some 'experts' working in local government, as the experience of health and highways engineers in the nineteenth century would indicate, the twentieth century has seen the development of a number of other professions relevant to the public sector generally and to local government particularly. This century has seen the emergence of such apparently powerful professions as town planning, housing manager, social worker, educational administrators and, most recently, recreation officer. In most cases, a national professional association seeks to control entry into the profession, by insisting that those working within the area should be members of the association, membership only being given to those who pass qualifying examinations, the standards of which are set by the association. The Royal Town Planning Institute in relation to planning or the British Association of Social Workers and social work provide examples.

Professionals such as these have been highly influential in determining both the kinds of policies adopted and the levels of services provided by many local authorities since 1945. Their influence and importance are derived from a number of sources. First, from their role as paid, technical experts. Whilst one may wish to argue the relative merits of individual welfare cases, it is difficult to dispute a highway engineer's design proposals for a particular road improvement scheme (though perhaps not so difficult to question the need for the improvement). Furthermore, we would argue that there has been an increasing tendency by local politicians to rely upon the advice of their experts even in those areas where the expertise is more apparent than real, such as recreation and leisure: the proliferation of leisure centres is perhaps a good example. The reluctance to question the professional's advice is partly due to the fact that most professionals are extremely well paid, so that questioning their advice may seem wasteful. But the influence and importance of the professionals is also derived from the fact that most councillors, including many committee chairmen and their deputies, are essentially little more than part-time paid amateurs. Only those with considerable length of service and detailed knowledge of their locality are likely to be in a position to be able to question their officers' advice intelligently, unless, that is, their own expertise is in the same area as that of the officials, something which is generally unlikely.

But the professionals' influence is reinforced by two other factors, both a reflection of the way in which the work of local authorities is structured. As with all large scale organisations (and even a district council today would qualify as one), local authorities operate in a bureaucratic fashion. That is to say, their work is organised in a hierarchical fashion, with responsibilities and duties allocated to appropriate levels. Thus much of the detailed work is done at several levels removed from chief officer level, so that he too may be less familiar with the details of some proposals made to committee and council than might be expected. But this hierarchical structure also gives the professionals a large degree of control over the information on which proposals are based. They know the best sources; they gather information in, they sift through and weed out a number of possible alternative policies. Furthermore, as a number of studies have shown, the officials are often able or even expected to control the *access* of members of the public and of organised groups to local councillors. In other words, the input of both individuals and groups to the policy-making system is likely to be via the officials rather than through the councillors.

Partly this is because of the hierarchical, bureaucratic nature of the system, but it is also a reflection of the trust which both councillors and the public have in the paid local government officials. Few of the textbooks, for example, place any great importance on the problem of corruption in local government, particularly among local officials, the reverberations of the Poulson and other affairs of the early 1970s notwithstanding. Trust of, or a belief in, the expert and his ability is perhaps another feature of post-war British politics, with the expectation that the experts will be able to find solutions to ever more complex problems. And this belief in the value of expertise is something which the various professions through their national associations have done much to promote, particularly through their stress on standards of service provision, their involvement in policy discussions and by their dissemination of information about current best practices. This would certainly be true of both land use and transport planning until the early 1970s and remains true of the health service today. Education is another example, in that much of the intellectual training of children takes place in schoolrooms where 'teacher knows best' and where parental involvement is generally at a minimum. In each of these cases, even if the professional has not claimed that the issues are matters of technical/professional competence, there is still a marked tendency, among councillors at least, to leave matters to the experts. And yet, as debates in planning, transportation and education all show, together with experience of all three, it is not always clear that the expert has provided the best solution, let alone the correct one, to many of the problems facing our communities today. Notwithstanding this point, however, many of the services under discussion had reached prescribed and accepted standards which were not in question, so that the professional officer's position was frequently not really questioned. The 1979 Conservative Government's concern with reducing public expenditure and narrowing the scope of government action meant that these standards (and here the professionals' position) could be questioned.

In talking about professionalism, an important distinction has to be made between those professionals who are essentially technocrats and those who are administrators. The former are those whose professionalism is derived from certain specific skills generally acquired by virtue of long periods of training: medicine and the law represent two classic examples, whilst town planning and social work are more recent ones. Administrators by contrast, owe their professional status to their position as *generalists*: administrative level civil servants in central government are one example; chief executives, with their Society of Local Authority Chief Executives (SOLACE), provide another example from the local government end of the spectrum. In the case of the latter, it could be argued that their expertise derives not only from their position as generalists but also because they are representatives of place, as well as being at the top of the local officers' hierarchy. Administrators are, by definition, fewer in number than their technocratic counterparts, and their training depends more on experience in post than on any formal imparting of skills.

In the case of the technocrats, it is clearly their specific skills and training which give rise to their expertise and to the claims made by their national associations for a role in the policy-making process, claims which it is difficult for government, both national and local to resist. Administrators, however, are in a different position, for it is not clear how either their role as generalists or their representation of place serves to give them any special claims to expertise, unless it be that their perspective allows them to develop a sense of priorities as and between policy arenas or within particular spatial areas. Nevertheless, the importance of paid officials in the policy-making and implementation processes raises questions of accountability and the ground rules by which they operate, rules which may not be a matter for debate. For example, one such rule may expect social workers to treat clients equitably, even though the clients may be unaware of these unwritten ground rules. In other cases some professional judgements, such as clinical decisions in health care, may be seen as inviolate and unquestionable: the expertise of the professional gives him an autonomy which is seen and accepted as legitimate. By contrast, there are other areas such as planning and transportation where professionals have laid claim to similar expertise, but subsequent political repercussions have led to a questioning of this claimed autonomy.

Given these different perspectives, various professionals are likely to have different attitudes towards participation and the part it should play in policy-making, even though what this discussion suggests is that public policy, on whatever subject, be it at the national or local level, has increasingly become the preserve of the paid official, excluding from policy discussions all but the most tenacious and competent of politicians and the most privileged of organised groups. Only those groups and individuals who are seen to be 'useful', or to have some sanction they can impose, or whose support may be necesary (in terms of policy implementation) (what we have called the 'consultees and major élites') are given access to the policy-making process. In other words, the spread of what Sharpe (1970) called incipient syndicalism has continued since he drew attention to its dangers in 1970. At that time he saw the participatory value of local government, both in terms of its elected members and of the wider opportunities for public participation which representative local government provided, as one of the major counters to the threats posed by the dominance of policy by professionals, particularly where they had either a high degree of autonomy or discretion.

Yet this professionalism has contributed, as have the other themes, to the last issue to be examined, namely the increasing remoteness of government, particularly local, from the people it serves. In this connection, local government reform in 1974 was a major contribution. Increasing the size of local authorities and reducing the number of elected members per authority or per number of population, must automatically weaken the relationship between the individual member of the public and his elected representative. The councillor has more constituents to deal with and a large area to cover: inevitably, even for the most assiduous councillor, contact with constituents must be more difficult than before reorganisation.

Physical distance from local authority offices also contributes to the remoteness of local government: council offices may simply be further away for many people, and then they may also be unwelcoming places when reached. The size and scope of local government business are also more complex and greater, hardly another inducement for people to become involved in policy matters, either of initiation or implementation. The complexity of many issues may apparently be beyond the competence of most individuals, who find themselves unable to find their way through the maze of explanations offered or regulations waved when they ask what they thought was an apparently simple question. Housing allocation procedures, welfare/social service regulations, improvement grant arrangements all provide examples where the apparently simple procedure of claiming one's rights might prove to be more complex than originally expected: how more complicated can these issues become when attempting to deal with strategic planning and transportation matters?

All this presumes that people are actually both interested and knowledgeable about the work of their local authority. The evidence on this matter is hardly optimistic, as far as it exists. Few people know the name of their local councillor, or can name who is responsible for particular services provided. Provided the service *appears* to be working and available when it is needed, few people seem willing to question whether it could be improved or whether it deals with the problems it is expected to solve. The disincentives to participation are great, even at the local government level. If this is true of the local level, it is equally so at the national level: government seems like a vast machine, steamrolling on regardless, or at least so some would have us believe. Mrs Thatcher's Government quickly dismantled some of the machine, cutting back on the range and scope of services for which government has increasingly been responsible. Thus, for example, as the 1980 Education Act shows, the Government reduced local authority responsibilities for school meals and gave greater freedom to charge for them, with the result that one authority, Lincoln, decided to stop providing school meals. Similarly, under the 1980 Housing Act, housing authorities are obliged to offer the houses for sale to tenants and were ordered to reduce council house building plans. The Local Government Act not only reduces local authority responsibilities in the planning field, but also gives central government greater control over individual local authorities' expenditure and borrowing programmes. A further reorganisation of the Health Service has been announced (July 1980), whilst quango cutting and the elimination of apparent waste are other activities in which Ministers have been involved.

These are all examples of the 1979 Conservative Government's cutback in the scope and range of governmental activity in Britain, particularly by reducing the level of public expenditure and hence the level of government borrowing: a crucial goal in the Government's economic strategy. But it also fits the Government's ideological preferences for a market-based society and one which encourages the virtue of self-help and self-discipline. This market philosophy, with its overtones of consumer choice and protection, poses a threat to participation in that it represents an alternative view of the relationship between the individual and the State. Instead of being directly involved in the process by which public policy is made and services delivered, the individual is expected to exercise choice in his consumption of services and to have his rights as a consumer protected by law. As such, it is participation in the consumption of public goods rather than their production. But such a philosophy could have the impact of making people react against government, particularly if cuts in public expenditure, rising unemployment and high levels of inflation continue unabated.

In a sense, the economic, social and political climate of the late 1970s and early 1980s has been more encouraging in terms of motivating participation than is perhaps true of the late 1960s and early 1970s when the political will to create a more participatory system of government was apparent. At that time there were a number of popular pressures which encouraged the introduction of more opportunities for participation in the policy-making process. First, there was the popular movement among (particularly) the young: the student participant culture of the 1960s, swinging London, the Paris May riots of 1968, the black riots and anti-Vietnam demonstrations in the United States at the time, all created a climate in which governments felt that the policy-making process had to be made more accessible, more open. Second, the late 1960s also produced doubts about the ability of experts to solve problems, particularly in the planning field, as well as concern with the long delays associated with the implementation of proposals. If those to be affected could be involved in the policy process and could be persuaded to give their support, then the process of implementing proposals could be speeded up. This was essentially the argument which underlay the 1965 Planning Advisory Group Report in the planning system and in part the Skeffington Committee Report on Public Participation in Planning. Third, there was also concern about the dominance in the policy process of both professionals and vested interests: by opening it up, not only would the policy process be made more accessible to all, thus reducing the influence of the major élites, but also perhaps the politicians, at both national and local level, might be able to wrest control over policy back from the bureaucracy, whose interests were undoubtedly better served by the closed decision-making process that characterises much of British government.

One issue at the centre of so much of the debate in the late 1960s and present again concerns the dissemination of information. Margaret Thatcher had promoted a private Act of Parliament in 1960 which had opened up local authority committee meetings to the press, whilst the 1964–70 Wilson Governments had also stressed the importance of publishing proposals and allowing access to information (open government was the phrase), introducing the idea of Green Papers and relaxing the fifty years' rule. These moves continued (but still marginally) under the Wilson/Callaghan Governments between 1974 and 1979, whilst the new Local Government Act lays considerable duties upon local authorities to publicise their activities and to inform the public about their work.

Similarly other legislation, such as the Town and Country Planning Act of 1968 together with that establishing General Improvement Areas and Housing Action Areas and dealing with major road proposals, encouraged or required local authorities to provide opportunities for people to make representations or to develop community-based groups which could contribute to the policy-making process. This kind of encouragement was developed most fully in the Urban Aid Programme, with its special emphasis on organising the non-participant and relatively deprived members of urban areas, particularly through the subsequently ill-fated Community Development Projects (CDPs).

These projects were ill-fated partly because of the extremely critical view they took of the causes of the problems with which they were expected to deal and the chances of success, but also because the resources given them by government and indeed those used for urban aid generally were very limited. Both of these factors strongly suggest that the motives of government in promoting public participation were concerned more with questions of social control than with encouraging widespread involvement in policy-making and implementation. Providing people with information about policies and securing a consensus of support for them would avoid many of the problems facing policy-makers, yet still leave them free to decide on the main policy lines. It would also create the important symbolic illusion of participation in government and perhaps permit the incorporation into the process of those often most critical of the existing processes.

Certainly this is the view of many radical critics of governmental attempts to increase public participation in both policy-making and service delivery, particularly at the local level. Radical groups concerned with promoting welfare rights, for example, often accuse other parts of the voluntary sector in the social services field with 'selling out' to those in positions of authority, seeing such groups as unable to bite the hand that feeds them. Many of the CDP groups felt they had faced similar problems, as do groups concerned with issues of racial discrimination. Suspicious of both the motives and acts of governments, such groups often continue their work on limited resources, perhaps outside the umbrella of the public sector, but not infrequently with some tacit or covert support from it. Such groups, which have increased in numbers in recent years, form part of the demand for participation from below. Pressures for participation have come not only from those in power, but also from numerous other popular groups, largely seeking opportunities either to express their views and to have them taken into account or else concerned that 'big government' should not trample over them. Others, mainly on the left, adopt a different stance, seeking to encourage increased public awareness of and involvement in the issues of the day. Couched in general terms, their appeals are to the working class either to seek to promote their share of the national public cake (the social wage) or the economic cake (increased wages) or else to protect themselves from attacks on their living standards through wage cuts and redundancies or reductions in welfare benefits. The TUC's 'Day of Action' in May 1980 is an example of this kind of appeal.

Still other critics, mainly those from the Continental Left such as Castells (1975) see the issue in even broader terms, suggesting that there exists an urban crisis over the increasing difficulty governments face in either maintaining the capitalist system (through intervention in the production sector) or making up for its deficiencies by extending the range of public goods provided under the title of collective consumption, such as health, education, housing and welfare services. Collective consumption, in Castell's view, is an essential part of the production of labour power, one of the main problems which the capitalist system faces. Given the increasing burden of financing the ever growing range of services provided, a crisis is seen as inevitable. The State, in both its central and local capacity, will be forced to reduce the level of collective services provided. In the face of these cuts, widespread opposition across class lines will grow, leading to the downfall of the capitalist system which is being bolstered up by the State through the provision of these collective goods and services.

Whilst it is possible to be critical of both the idea of collective consumption and of the real possibility of new urban protest movements developing across class lines (Saunders, 1979), there can be little doubt that the late 1970s (and particularly from 1979) saw considerable reductions in the level of state expenditures on public goods and services. It is also likely that the cuts in public expenditure fell most heavily on those least able to handle the burden or most in need of public goods. In most cases, cuts in housing, education and welfare services fall most heavily on working class people, whilst the middle class can make alternative provision in many cases. Middle class mothers, for example, may be able to provide a better packed lunch or to collect their children at lunch time when school meals prove either too costly or are no longer provided by an education authority desperate to make expenditure cuts.

Concern over levels of public expenditure and the need for it to be reduced is, of course, also very much an issue for critics from the Right of the political spectrum. Only by reducing public expenditure can levels of taxation be cut so as to allow firms to retain more of their profits. In turn, given greater profits, firms will be more willing to invest, thus creating more jobs, which in turn will raise incomes. People will spend more on goods and services privately produced, thus increasing these firms' profits . . . and so, in theory at least, the process continues, with greater economic growth leading to increases in the people's standards of living. Again working and middle classes would benefit, as they did under the relatively prosperous years of the late 1950s and early 1960s. The capitalist miracle will have been worked yet again.

Such a view, like that of the Left, probably discourages participation rather than the reverse, if only because both perspectives have something of an unreal air about them. Both perspectives, however, mask an issue which is of concern, and to which we shall return later, namely as to whether or not there is a mobilisation of bias in British politics, both national and local, a bias which, in terms of this book, encourages governments to provide services largely at the behest of certain groups and interests (the middle classes), and that those who benefit most or suffer least from the provision of public goods and services are those same groups and interests. It is, for example, possible to argue that many of the changes which have led to an opening up of the local policy-making processes, or which have led to considerable service expansion since the mid-1960s were instigated by the middle-class organised interests. Indeed, in terms of being remote from government, it might be argued that it has been essentially the middle classes who have been 'excluded' from influence in post-war British politics and the working classes, by contrast, are no less remote from (and may indeed have greater influence over) government now than they were fifty or a hundred years ago. As a result, most of the attempts by government to involve people in local service provision have been designed to reincorporate the middle classes, giving them back the access, the proximity, the sense of legitimising influence, which many of the middle class may think is their rightful place in politics. But this is a theme to which we shall return after having reviewed more closely the growing experience of public participation in a number of local services. We begin this review, however, by examining participation which is community or neighbourhood based: that is, it has a spatial, rather than a functional, basis.

Public participation in local services is affected not only by the nature of those services, but also by the location or scale of the provision. People show a much greater interest in matters directly affecting them in their immediate neighbourhood than they do in the wider affairs of a local authority. Yet the importance of neighbourhood for community feeling has become recognised at a time when there has been pressure for local authorities to become larger for political or managerial reasons. Larger local authorities are presumed to command superior resources which can be more equitably distributed over a wider area than is the case with smaller units. In recent years the relationship between scale and efficiency in the provision of local services has been challenged; but the Royal Commissions on Local Government in the 1960s were impressed by the arguments favouring increased size, and the reorganisation of 1974 reflected their attitudes in this respect.

Although local authorities have become larger, and consequently more remote from the people they serve, the impact of the services provided continues to be manifested at a local level – a primary school catchment area, for example, or the area of a local plan. When this occurs, the functional needs of the service and the level at which people are willing to respond come closer together. People express their interest by creating action groups formed either round a particular service or with a general concern for a very localised area, while some local authorities experiment with neighbourhood management schemes to co-ordinate provision at the point of service delivery. Such proposals for area management usually stress the possibility of encouraging public participation at the neighbourhood level, although the rhetoric is not always matched by the reality.

A discussion of neighbourhood participation, therefore, is often concerned with managerial efficiency and the correct level to engage certain political questions, as well as with the most likely location of popular involvement. These different perspectives have led to developments in neighbourhood organisation in the past decade: but the varied objectives being pursued have often led to confusion and sometimes to conflict. In this chapter we shall consider three of these approaches. First, there are the neighbourhood action groups that seek to influence the existing political process. By putting pressure on their representatives they try to obtain decisions favourable to their own point of view. Many groups of residents or tenants act in this way. Second, there are attempts to integrate neighbourhood involvement into the representative system. Community councils associated with area-based management are an obvious example of this approach. Third, there are the neighbourhood or community councils which balance the representative institutions by providing a participatory infrastructure independent of the local authorities. Each of these developments will be considered in turn, but first we need to consider a little further the understanding of community that has informed the debate.

Community is one of the most difficult concepts in the language of sociology and political science. In its most general form it implies a shared identity or common interest which may be based upon almost any characteristic. We speak of the Catholic community or the black community; and in another context there is a community of chamber music enthusiasts. In this chapter we are concerned with the shared interest which is believed to occur among people who live in the same locality. The reasons given for this shared interest vary with the perspective of the commentator. The early work of the Institute of Community Studies in East London frequently stressed the importance of family and friendship ties in maintaining the daily social interaction which forms the basis of community life. Other community studies have emphasised the importance of a perceived threat from planning developments or elsewhere in defining an area for community action. Despite these differences in interpretation we may accept that most people find comfort in familiar surroundings. We are all more relaxed and self-confident when we are on our 'home ground'. The question is whether these social feelings of community can be related to the provision of local services.

In 1969 the Royal Commission on Local Government in England commissioned a survey into community attitudes to examine, among other things, 'the geographical size of community areas, particularly in relation to the existing boundaries of local authority areas' (Community Attitudes Survey 1969). They used the concept of a 'home area' and asked respondents to describe the limits of the area surrounding their house within which they felt 'at home'. A separate survey was conducted in Scotland for the Royal Commission on Local Government in Scotland. The survey results supported the view that people were aware of the spatial limits of their neighbourhood. Nearly four out of five respondents were able to conceptualise a 'home area' and most described it in physical terms by reference to street patterns or local landmarks. The areas described often encompassed only a few streets in urban areas and about three-quarters were smaller than an electoral ward in extent.

About half the people interviewed expressed an interest in events occurring in the 'home areas'. These events, of course, might be concerned with personal affairs: the births, marriages and deaths which are the staple of many local newspapers. But the events might also be concerned with local authority activities affecting the area: the closure of a local school, for example, or new road proposals.

Although people are interested in local events they are not knowledgeable about the existing political institutions in the locality. In another survey based on the Royal Commission's questionnaire one of the present authors found that although the degree of attachment to the home area was related to the interest expressed in local events, it was not correlated with an awareness of the name of the local councillor or of the ward he represented. Hampton's results suggested the need for new types of local institutions if the interest in events occurring in the home area was to be linked with participation in the provision of local services (Hampton 1970: 119–21, 301–2).

The development of institutions corresponding to the needs expressed in the previous paragraphs is inhibited by several factors. First, there is the very complexity of the concept of community feeling. Surveys deal in averages and tendencies, but the focus of the perception of community varies from individual to individual, and may vary for any individual at different times in the life cycle. Young people will have different points of reference within their community from those of married couples, and the elderly will have yet another perspective. Community feeling, in other words, is specific, localised, changeable, and many-layered: people constantly respond in different ways to the social needs expressed through their interaction with their neighbours. The needs of most forms of administrative organisation for continuity, order and settled boundaries conflict with the kaleidoscope of community feeling.

Even if boundaries are drawn round areas containing clusters of community perceptions such as primary school catchment areas, polling districts and so on, the great variety in the size of such areas from one locality to another makes it impossible to create uniform units of administration corresponding to community feeling (Lowe 1977). There is a mismatch, therefore, between the functional needs of most local authority services and the scale of area organisation which would encourage more people to participate in the discussion or control of such services. And there is yet another problem. People tend to be interested in particular services at different times: education when their children are attending school; planning when their neighbourhood is affected; health or social services when their relatives are in need.

These difficulties in relating community feeling to the social and administrative needs of service provision have prevented the emergence of a clear-cut, uniform system of neighbourhood participation. We have instead a bewildering array of voluntary, statutory and quasi-statutory organisations whose relevance to participation is more often assumed than demonstrated.

NEIGHBOURHOOD ACTION

Neighbourhood action groups and council tenants' associations share the community characteristic of being based on a defined residential area. They are frequently formed to protect the community from a perceived threat, whether in the form of planned redevelopment in the case of the action groups or of rent increases in the case of tenants' associations. When organisations are formed in response to an outside threat then the perception of community is consequent upon these extraneous sources and not upon a social or personal view of community. Thus many action group boundaries are defined by the area of a local plan, and tenants' associations are usually based on housing estates subject to similar ranges of rent increase. Sometimes the planning authority or housing authority may itself stimulate the formation of an action group or tenants' association in order to have a regular channel of communication with local people. At times of conflict between the local authority and local people, over council house rent increases for example, these 'official' associations may be opposed by 'independent' organisations formed to contest a particular issue.

Conflict between rival groups based on the same neighbourhood area is not confined to these cases. Action groups may be found in affluent suburbs or in areas of terraced working-class housing; but often the uniformity of interest among local residents will not be as uniform as the compact nature of most action group areas would suggest. Many action groups are in areas of mixed nineteenth- and early twentieth-century housing. In some cases owner-occupiers may be protecting a relatively low building density against redevelopment, or seeking to prevent a substantial change from family residences to multi-occupancy or commercial use. Underlying the broad appeals to community feeling there is often the sharp incentive of property values. In one classic case an association formed to promote environmental improvements in Barnsbury, North London, was opposed by an action group of long-standing working-class residents who were being disadvantaged by the consequent 'gentrification' of the neighbourhood (Ferris 1972).

Action groups vary considerably in the methods they adopt to to be representative. First, they must demonstrate their ability to speak for all local residents, or at least for a substantial majority of them. Second, they must convince a local authority that the views of their neighbourhood deserve greater attention than those of less well-organised areas.

Actions groups vary considerably in the methods they adopt to establish their legitimacy as representatives of their areas. Some action groups have elaborate organisational structures with registered memberships paying subscriptions and electing officers and committees for different purposes; other groups are far more informal. It is common for an action group to assume that everyone within the area is a member. The group may have started from the enthusiasm of a public meeting and the volunteers who then formed a committee remain the public voice for the area for many years. New members are co-opted as vacancies occur or activists arrive in the area. Smaller action groups are often based on areas bearing a resemblance to the 'home areas' described in the surveys mentioned earlier: a few streets, or a patch of housing defined by surrounding industry or physical boundaries like roads or railway lines. If the area chosen is wider than this, perhaps in response to a planning initiative of the local authority, then there may be a network of street groups as the basis of the organisation. This intimate scale makes possible such devices as a door-to-door canvass to solicit views on particular policies.

Despite the obvious advantages of public demonstrations of

accountability, some groups degenerate into closed coteries who paternalistically assume that their views are in the best interests of their neighbours. In this they may often be right. In dealing with very small local activities of this kind we must beware of transferring the expectations of formal representative democracy into an inappropriate setting. The self-appointed street leader may have visited every house. Informal meetings in a corner shop or public house, together with chance discussions on the pavement, may provide closer accountability than the most elaborate election procedure.

In addition to expressing the views of local people on controversial issues, groups fulfil other functions which enable them to gain an understanding of local needs. They also provide an opportunity for self-help in meeting these needs. A wide range of facilities is provided including playgroups, luncheon clubs for the elderly or handicapped, youth clubs, recreational and cultural events and advice bureaux. The list could be extended almost indefinitely. The smaller groups, of course, may provide only one or two additional services for their area, but some of the larger groups provide sufficient services for them to be considered as embryo neighbourhood councils.

This development of community self-help is the modern counterpart of 'neighbouring'. Changes in family life and increased geographical mobility have led to a dispersion of the tight-knit communities described in many early sociological studies. The responsibilities of the extended family or good neighbour have been taken over by the growing social work professions. This growth in professionalism does not always provide an improved service and much current professional thinking refers to the importance of developing 'community care'. Once again the needs of local service administration and the interests of local people meet at the neighbourhood level.

Action groups which provide a range of services, sometimes with local authority support, gain in status in their negotiations over more controversial matters. They may also modify their demands so that their existing relationships are not jeopardised. The advantages and disadvantages of a more complex relationship with the local authority will depend upon the issues being contested and the political viewpoint of the commentator. But certainly co-operative relationships developed in the provision of services can change the nature of more overtly political disagreements.

Tenants' associations are a particular form of residents' group, but the different name is indicative of a different emphasis in their activities. Usually they are formed by local authority tenants, but there are some organisations for private tenants. The Housing Corporation is actively encouraging tenant involvement in the management of housing associations and this implies some form of tenant organisation. Tenants' associations are frequently created, or grow stronger, at times of conflict over rent policies, and become quiescent when the issues are settled. During the quiet periods some associations assist individual tenants in their approaches to the local authority, or make collective suggestions about repairs and other matters affecting the estates, but such activity is rarely pursued with vigour or continuity. More often, especially if a tenants' hall is available, there is a continuing responsibility for social functions which are a means of keeping an association together. At these social events the officers are often available to give advice to individual members, but tenants' associations seldom provide the more sophisticated social and welfare services attempted by the larger action groups. They are more in the tradition of trade unions negotiating about terms and conditions of services than in the spirit of community self-help. Nevertheless, there is now some interest in involving council tenants more fully in the management of their own estates and we shall consider such developments in Chapter 6.

Action groups provide continuing evidence that interest in local affairs extends far beyond the small numbers willing to stand for election to local authorities, but this interest is not equally well organised throughout a local authority area. Opponents of the groups frequently see them as a way of mobilising neighbourhood bias and as an irritant in a local authority policy-making process seeking to allocate resources fairly throughout the area. Such arguments are frequently put forward by councillors during the conflicts which occur between action groups and local authorities. There is sometimes justification for this attitude, as the Barnsbury case illustrates, but action groups are too heterogeneous for easy generalisations. Over the past decade they have introduced a further participatory dimension into local politics in many cities: sometimes in opposition, but sometimes in close co-operation with local authority departments.

The diversity both in the organisational forms adopted by the groups, and in the range of functions that they fulfil, reinforces the importance of flexibility in providing for participatory activity. However many services they provide, action groups are not local authorities writ small: they are the spontaneous expression of local feeling about specific topics, in specific localities, at specific times. As such, they ebb and flow with the tide of public opinion and interest.

NEIGHBOURHOOD MANAGEMENT AND COMMUNITY DEVELOPMENT

About the same time as the action groups were beginning to develop, the Government became interested in neighbourhood involvement. The Royal Commission on Local Government was established against a backcloth of dissatisfaction with existing administrative arrangements, and in the context of a prognosis of a deterioration in conditions in many urban areas. The potential breakdown of order and authority in the cities was seen as a threat following the urban violence in America in the late 1960s. One factor in the declining morale of the inner suburbs was believed to be the remoteness of government from the people. The consequences were seen as apathy and alienation: the solution proposed was a greater measure of public participation. As we shall notice in subsequent chapters, several of the reports into particular public services included appropriate recommendations.

The interest in public participation was paralleled by the growing interest in corporate management. The inner cities were referred to as areas of multiple deprivation: co-ordination of service delivery at this level was seen as one method of overcoming the problems of particular neighbourhoods. In 1969 the Home Office sponsored twelve Community Development Projects in small, closely defined urban areas. They were based on the twin beliefs that a concentration of effort in a small area would raise both the level of service provision, and the capacity of people to benefit from the services available. The involvement of local people was, therefore, an integral part of the strategy adopted.

Once appointed the projects pursued a classic community development approach: they studied the social and economic structure of their areas, and encouraged large numbers of local self-help initiatives. But their attitudes towards the causes of the problems of the inner cities, and consequently of the possible solutions, steadily moved away from the Government's original conception. The Community Development Projects began to emphasise the structural causes of poverty and the role of the declining urban areas in the overall pattern of national economic policy. With this analysis, the problems of the inner cities could not be solved within the neighbourhoods most affected: changes were necessary in the system as a whole. Local participation in the provision of services was increasingly seen as irrelevant by the Community Development Projects unless it led to a consciousness of the need for radical social change. This was a path the Government had no intention of taking and the projects ended amidst a controversy which concealed the considerable contribution they had made both to the theory and practice of community work.

Despite the traumas of the Community Development Projects, the Government has continued experiments which link the concept of neighbourhood to the solving of urban problems. The Inner Area Studies in Birmingham, Liverpool and Southwark placed more emphasis on local authority management than the Community Development Projects, but they were also concerned to promote neighbourhood community involvement. The conclusions from these studies were calmer in tone than the reports from the Community Development Projects, but the message was the same: large-scale social problems cannot be solved in small-scale areas.

Even if the neighbourhood is not the most appropriate level to tackle major urban problems, there is still a need for the larger local authorities to develop ways in which they can take more account of the different localities within their areas. In September 1974, the Department of the Environment announced support for trials of neighbourhood management in several local authority areas and the schemes began to be monitored by the Institute of Local Government Studies in June 1976. The emphasis is on sensitive management but there is a strong recognition of the importance of enhancing the part played by the community in meeting neighbourhood needs. Neighbourhood management is, therefore, the management face of a coin which has neighbourhood councils on its other side: several local authorities have introduced such councils as a concomitant of area-based management schemes.

The first interim report from the monitoring team describes six schemes providing examples of several different approaches to area-based management. Stockport is the most interesting for the theme of this chapter as it covers the whole of the local authority area and includes provision for a system of community councils. The following description is taken from the interim report. Stockport is divided into three administrative areas, each of which has an area office housing an Area Co-ordinator and his staff. The Area Co-ordinator is responsible for providing some services and for aiding the co-ordination of others. He is also responsible for advice and information services to the public. These are available from area offices.

The council has appointed eight Area Committees which fit within the three administrative areas. These are full committees of the council but do not have a budget or executive powers. They cover two or three wards and include all the ward councillors together with one or two county councillors. The committees may consider any aspect of council policy or administration affecting their area and may make recommendations and proposals to any other committee.

Community involvement is sought through a system of twenty-two community councils and by contact with other local groups and voluntary associations. There is at least one community development officer in each of the three administrative areas to assist in this work. The monitoring team (C.J. Horn *et al*. 1977: 8) describes the relationship between the community councils and the local authority:

The Council applies certain criteria by which it will determine whether a community council should be 'recognised' or not. These include statements as to their non-party political nature, their intentions to work with the authority 'to ensure all available resources are brought to bear for the benefit of the community', and their intention to present the local authority with a representative community view on matters on which it is consulted. Annual public meetings are held at which all residents over eighteen years may vote and stand for election. A recognised community council is entitled to a special relationship with the Council which will include the right to meet with the relevant area committee every six months, and to receive copies of all agendas and reports of area committees together with council minutes. They may send representatives to the area committee when matters of particular importance to them are being discussed. They will also receive some financial aid from the Council.

Neighbourhood management, as the name implies, is concerned with administrative efficiency. The various officers and committees concerned have an advisory rather than an executive function and in general there has not been any change in the existing methods of taking decisions through the normal methods of political pressure and argument. This creation of formal forums for wider public debate of public issues can be seen as a democratic advance, but it can also be interpreted as a method of co-opting dissent. Cynthia Cockburn describes neighbourhood councils as the tender aspect of tough-minded corporate management (Cockburn 1977). Nowhere is this approach more plausible than in the area management trials, but neighbourhood or community councils are more diverse than any simplistic analysis might suggest.

NEIGHBOURHOOD AND COMMUNITY COUNCILS

The description neighbourhood or community council covers many different organisations: voluntary bodies; the councils associated with neighbourhood management; and statutory institutions based on formal representative elections. At the latter end of the spectrum they are often referred to as 'urban parish councils'.

This similarity of size and title between neighbourhood and parish councils is more confusing than enlightening for the basis in the community of the two types of institution is quite different. In rural areas in England parish councils represent populations varying from a few hundreds to many thousands: most, but by no means all, are related to areas which share a sense of communal identity. The parishes are generally small, clearly distinguished from their neighbours, and can often trace their existence back through the centuries. They are part of the statutory system of local government and as such hold formal elections, provide various services, and have the power to levy a rate through precepting the district authority. They are a part of the representative democratic system. Neighbourhood councils on the contrary, rest for their authority on a participatory view of democracy.

The potential advantages of parishes as an opportunity for popular participation at a truly local level have caused a renewal of interest in recent years. The Local Government Act 1972, removed the regulations limiting parish council expenditure and granted them the right to be consulted on all planning applications in their areas. This strengthening of the role of parish councils was in line with the views of the Royal Commission on Local Government in England who had become, '... increasingly convinced by those who emphasised the need for an organ of community at grass-roots level' (Royal Commission on Local Government 1969: Vol. I, para. 12).

The Royal Commission wanted the system extended into the urban areas, but neither the Labour nor the Conservative Government felt able to face this additional complication in the already difficult matter of local government reorganisation in England. The Local Government Act 1972, introduced community councils in Wales (subsequent legislation also introduced them in Scotland), but in England a few successor parish councils in the place of

45

absorbed urban districts were the only response to the recommendations for 'grass-roots' councils. The large urban areas remained unprovided for in this respect.

The community councils in Wales and Scotland owed more to the Minority Report prepared by Mr Derek Senior than to the Royal Commission Report itself. Mr Senior proposed the introduction of 'common councils' drawing on the experience of the 'communes' existing in other European countries. A common council would only exist where there was a local demand and 'would have nothing to do with the running of statutory services' (Royal Commission on Local Government 1969: Vol. II, para. 430). Such councils would, therefore, be quite different from parish councils. They would add a new participatory dimension to local government rather than become part of the representative system.

The reorganisation of local government in Scotland reduced over 400 administrative units to 65: 9 regional councils, 53 district councils, and 3 island councils. The community councils were intended, in part, to offset the remoteness of this new system. They were not intended to be a 'third tier' of local government and have not been given any statutory functions. The aim was to create a type of organisation which could turn its attention to anything of concern to the local community. A community council can do anything not expressly prohibited by law, whereas a local authority must be able to show positive authorisation for its actions in statute. During the parliamentary debate on the Local Government (Scotland) Act, the Under-Secretary of State for Scotland described the Government's attitude towards community councils: 'In other words we are looking for the best of both worlds – the freedom of a voluntary association combined with the unquestioned status of the representative body for the neighbourhood.' The responsibility for discovering this happy coincidence was left to the district councils in consultation with the general public.

The formation of the Scottish community councils has been monitored by Michael Masterson on behalf of the Scottish Development Department (Masterson 1978). 'Excluding Edinburgh', where the district council refused to prepare a scheme, he found, '1,288 community councils were proposed in Scotland . . . ninety-one per cent of them have populations less than 10,000 . . . if all the councils were formed and all the places filled, there could be twelve times as many directly elected community councillors as there are district and islands councillors'. By the middle of 1978 nearly nine out of ten possible community councils had been formed. The number of candidates coming forward was sufficient for the places available in most cases although contests only occurred in about one-third of the areas. Contests were sometimes avoided when potential candidates withdrew in favour of neighbours or friends: they are *that* kind of election. The political parties have been interested but have not formally contested the seats. In general the degree of interest has been comparable to that shown in parish councils in England.

During their first year in existence the community councils tackled a great variety of jobs: commenting on local plans, cleaning up their area, dealing with traffic problems, organising carol services and other social events, protesting about bus routes, and becoming involved in the many other neighbourhood activities so typical of residents' groups and parish pump politics. Some community councils produce newsletters and some hold open meetings where it is difficult to tell the members of the council from the other people attending. The whole style of operation is different from the service providing local authorities.

These developments in Scotland have no counterpart in England, although there has been considerable discussion of the possibilities. In February 1970, an Association of Neighbourhood Councils was sponsored by a distinguished group of people including Mr Senior and leading members of all three major parties. In addition to pressing for statutory provision the Association encouraged the establishment of non-statutory neighbourhood councils. By 1974 it estimated that there 'are now some 200 neighbourhood or community councils in unparished areas of England'. To be included in this list councils had both to arrange their own activities such as helping with elderly people or children, and to make representations to the local authority and other bodies on matters affecting their locality. The number quoted is likely to be an underestimate. The Association received a limited response to its survey both from local authorities who were asked to provide lists of organisations and from approximately 6,500 organisations finally identified. Only 1,600 replied to the questionnaire from which the selection was made of 224 'neighbourhood councils'.

The response to the Royal Commission report by the two major parties was based on practical expediency: there was not the time available to introduce thousands of community councils in England. In principle, 'grass-roots' institutions were supported and the continued growth of neighbourhood action groups – to say nothing of the success of Liberal 'community politics' – kept the question to the fore. In opposition, Mr Wilson, then leader of the parliamentary Labour party, supported the idea of neighbourhood councils and soon after it returned to power in 1974 the Labour government issued a Consultation Paper. The Paper suggested making statutory status available to neighbourhood organisations in areas where local support was forthcoming. The councils would have formal rights of consultation with local authorities over certain planning matters and could attract other participatory responsibilities. Statutory status would provide access to limited financial support from public funds, and this in turn would require some form of public accountability through elections. On all these matters the Paper was careful to set out various possibilities upon which comment was invited.

Despite ministerial support, the Consultation Paper was received with favour neither by local authorities nor by many citizens' groups. The local authorities opposed another layer of elected councils as an unnecessary complication to an already complex system. Citizens' groups were afraid of being co-opted through statutory status into a system whose attitudes they did not share. They wished to maintain the flexibility and non-party political character that voluntary effort allowed them to develop. The Association for Neighbourhood Councils welcomed the Consultation Paper and urged support for legislation but in this respect it appeared to be in a minority even among those who supported 'grass-roots' participation in the neighbourhood. By this time the Association appeared to have lost sight of the vital distinctions between consultation, formal representative democracy, and participatory action. Its publications supported such diverse institutions as the Stockport Community Councils and campaigning voluntary neighbourhood organisations without discussing the different functions such groups can fulfil in the local political process. Their emphasis on statutory status as the only method of ensuring authority for neighbourhood groups in their relations with local councils was being overtaken by the more direct participatory approach of the groups themselves.

As part of the official interest in neighbourhood councils the Department of the Environment commissioned Jennifer Talbot and Stephen Humble to study more closely the organisations identified in the Association of Neighbourhood Councils' survey. Talbot and Humble specified that a neighbourhood council should cover a defined area with an electorate between 3,000 and 15,000; it should be democratically elected by all those on the electoral register; and it should make representations on behalf of the local community to outside bodies. Only fifteen fulfilled these stringent criteria for a fully fledged neighbourhood council; although this may only indicate that the criteria were inappropriate. The major difficulty which occurred was with the idea of democratic elections. Many of the original 224 restricted voting to those who paid a membership fee; these organisations were excluded by Talbot and Humble from their list. If the requirement of open voting by those on the electoral register had been relaxed then 70 per cent would have qualified. Even among the select fifteen the formal democratic procedures were not strong: only three held ballot elections; usually the election was at an annual general meeting. Without statutory backing it is difficult and expensive for voluntary organisations to organise a full ballot of a neighbourhood, but these figures suggest that other methods are usually found acceptable even among the strongest neighbourhood organisations.

The more fully developed neighbourhood councils as defined by Talbot and Humble were usually closely linked with their local authorities upon whom they were dependent for funds, staff support and headquarters. Their budgets were usually contained within a range between £200 and £2,000; where larger sums were involved these went to the running of local services. Talbot and Humble considered the neighbourhood councils to be 'well-behaved' bodies, effective in pursuing their activities, but making little impact either on local councillors' attitudes or on public apathy. Such conclusions highlight the hesitations felt by many community activists and help to explain why the Association for Neighbourhood Councils found itself isolated in its response to the 1974 Consultation Paper.

CONCLUSION

The readiness with which people respond to events in their own locality has made the neighbourhood an attractive level of organisation both for innovatory local government management and for radical activists. The radicals hope that the immediacy of local issues will stimulate actions leading to a growth of class consciousness: the locality is the venue of struggle rather than its purpose. The non-radical approach is less precise in its objectives: neighbourhood participation may contribute to many policies – some political in purpose and some managerial. It may be hoped either that neighbourhood activity will reduce alienation from existing institutions – the counterbalance to the expectations of the radicals –

or that neighbourhood conditions can be ameliorated by local management, an amelioration that may prove both more effective and cheaper through the participation of voluntary organisations.

These varying expectations and perspectives are often present in an individual organisation which struggles to represent its locality and to provide some neighbourhood services within the normal political context of differing opinions. The potential tension is apparent. Despite these difficulties, studies of existing neighbourhood activities contain some hopeful conclusions. First, neighbourhood groups are not as open to manipulation either by radical activists or by the managerial establishment as each side publicly fears. By and large, people pursue their own interests with the degree of moderation or anger appropriate to the issue: extraneous manipulation soon leads to atrophy as the membership of the organisation withers away. This is one reason why a large and active membership may be a more effective guarantee of the representative nature of an organisation than formal provisions for ballots on the basis of the electoral roll.

Second, there does appear to be a possibility of increasing public participation in local affairs by the establishment of some form of neighbourhood organisation intermediate between the single-issue pressure group and a service-providing local authority. Both the growth of neighbourhood groups and the successful establishment of the Scottish community councils support this view. But as yet the concept is not clearly defined and its relationship to the management of services is uncertain. For many politicians the idea of a neighbourhood organisation which is concerned with, but not of, local government is difficult to understand. Quite properly they see the broad determination of policy and the allocation of resources as the crucial content of politics. They complain of parochialism when most people persist in being interested, if at all, only in extremely local manifestations of public policy, and in the social events and concerns of their neighbourhood. During the debate on local government reorganisation in Scotland many Members of Parliament seemed bewildered by the establishment of community councils without defined responsibilities for services. Their attitude is shared by many councillors in both Scotland and the rest of Britain. The idea of a neighbourhood council linking the participatory initiatives of the public with the representative functions of a local authority is seldom discussed because it is so little understood.

Finally, we are left with an open question: whether it would be better to encourage neighbourhood activity by statutory provision, as in Scotland, or by the increased activity of community workers, or by some other methods. Neighbourhood activities share the twin-faced characteristic of Janus, the god of doors and gates. One aspect faces the social involvement which enhances life in a well-known locality; the other aspect faces the political process. The gateway between them is opened by a neighbourhood organisation, but movement often remains difficult as the means appropriate to one sphere prove inappropriate in the other. A solution to this problem could prove of considerable importance for those who wish to encourage public participation.

Chapter four
STATUTORY PARTICIPATION IN PLANNING

Statutory participation was introduced in 1968 into a field of local government which was not sixty years old. Yet planning had grown from a relatively simple enterprise designed to combat problems of the urban working class, to become a highly technical and complex procedure for producing strategic and comprehensive proposals. The scale of planning became increasingly large and its control more centralised, particularly after 1947. A planning profession emerged to meet the demands of this development but did not always find it easy to establish a clear identity for itself. It came to be seen by the public as both unjustifiably visionary and mystifyingly technological, as well as unwilling to accept its manifest, political responsibilities.

Opportunities for direct public involvement in the planning process had been very few. The principal route in the 1950s and 1960s – the right of objection by affected parties at public inquiry – was restricted to very few participants. Inquiries became semi-judicial and alienating in their form. From an administrative viewpoint, they were increasingly an unwieldy instrument and distracted government from basic issues of policy. For the general public, inquiries confused the question of balance between public and private interests and, while appearing to offer promise of participation, fulfilled nobody's expectations. Reviews of the planning system by the Planning Advisory Group (1965) and by Dobry (1975) drew attention to these and other shortcomings.

By the 1970s some form of public involvement was routinely practised with the major experience being concentrated at structure plan level. But we shall see that the geographical and temporal scope of structure planning, its comprehensive and abstract nature made it an unlikely vehicle for popular participation. The question of balance between individual and group participation remained unresolved. Participation tended to be interpreted by planners as another field for purely technical exercise. The emphasis was on mastery of the most efficient techniques for disseminating information. If a public response was energetically solicited, it was often done through highly specialised sample survey.

THE STATUTORY PROVISIONS

It is convenient to identify the introduction of statutory public participation with the 1968 Town and Country Planning Act. The transition is not clear-cut, however. Members of the public had some statutory rights to involvement in the planning process before 1968; in particular, the right to make objections or representations in certain kinds of planning inquiry. The provisions of the 1968 Act made possible the development of participatory planning, rather than directly enjoining it. The enactment (T & CP Act 1968, 3(i) has been criticised as unduly vague:

... the local planning authority shall take such steps as will in their opinion secure
   (a) that adequate publicity is given in their area to the report of Survey ... and to the matters which they propose to include in the plan;
   (b) that persons who may be expected to desire an opportunity of making representations to the authority with respect to those matters are made aware that they are entitled to an opportunity of doing so; and
   (c) that such persons are given an adequate opportunity of making such representations;
and the authority shall consider any representations made to them within the prescribed period.

A more specific view of what participation might entail, within the terms of the Act, can be found in the report (1969) of the Skeffington Committee. It highlighted the policy behind the Act, by citing from the White Paper (Town and Country Planning): 'One of the Government's main aims in the present review of planning legislation is to ensure that there are greater opportunities for the discussion of important changes while they are still at the formative stage and can be influenced by the people whose lives they will affect.' Skeffington stressed that information-giving by the local authority and the opportunity to comment is not the whole of participation. It also includes taking an active part throughout the planning process and sharing in the formulation of policies and proposals. It was felt by the Committee that participation 'can improve the quality of decisions by public authorities and give personal satisfaction to those affected by the decision.' It was recognised that the public was a heterogeneous body. The report gave more detailed advice on techniques than was otherwise available to local authorities from central government.

The historical context

However, the 1968 provisions for participation, cannot be seen by themselves. They are part of a historical process which began formally with the Town Planning Act of 1909. This early Act dealt principally with public health and housing policies – issues which we shall treat separately in later chapters. It contained nothing of the concepts of overall strategies and comprehensive planning which we now associate with town and country planning. There was no planning profession to produce the schemes it envisaged; the work of existing local authority employees, architects, surveyors and public health officials was merely extended. The significance of the Act was in enlisting land-use control to combat a major social problem – the condition of the urban working class.

Subsequent Acts (in 1919 and 1932) took the process further. After the First World War any authority with a population of more than 20,000 had to produce development plans. This was later extended to compulsory and comprehensive schemes for nearly all non-agricultural land. But planning between the wars was largely a failure. Much of it devolved on the district councils which were too small, weak and, particularly, too numerous to tackle the major problems of rapid urbanisation. There was a decline in agriculture and the quality of the countryside and a growing imbalance between town and country. The need to co-ordinate housing and industrial development overstrained the powers for co-operation of neighbouring authorities. At the centre, the Ministry of Health did little other than protect the rights of property-owners against unfair treatment by local authorities. In practice there was little effective control over development in the 1930s, and increasing dissatisfaction with the planning system's inability to deal with the major problems. The system's failings during this period already indicated a need for comprehensive planning and a greater degree of centralisation.

It was the Second World War which provided the motivation to change the system. Quite apart from the physical destruction which needed repair, there was a belief that 'planning' had worked in the conduct of the war. New ideas were more acceptable and administrators were prepared to innovate. The need for a central authority and for some form of regional planning was recognised. The time seemed ripe for the birth of a new profession which could undertake some of the responsibilities of restructuring post-war Britain.

The 1947 Town and Country Planning Act introduced machinery for the comprehensive planning of all land in England and Wales, by development plans which were to provide a combination of strategy and projection over a twenty year period. A degree of central control was incorporated. Approval from the Ministry of Town and Country Planning was required for plans. Individuals and organisations had the right of appeal to the Ministry against refusals of planning applications to develop; and where undesirable permissions had been granted, they could be 'called-in' by the Ministry, with the possible sanction against the local authority of having to compensate the would-be developer.

Planning was now to be the task primarily of county and county borough councils; partly with the hope of avoiding the difficult relations between the many different and smaller authorities of the pre-war period. The power to delegate planning functions to a lower tier authority was variously used; though in 1958 the Local Government Act enabled authorities with a population of more than 60,000 to require delegation to them.

Individuals and organisations were more directly affected by the 1947 legislation than hitherto. For most developments they now needed planning permission, rather than simply having to keep within broad and often unenforceable zoning regulations. They could appeal to the Minister if permission were not granted; and in many cases this gave them the opportunity to present their case at a local public inquiry. However, statutory involvement in planning was restricted to the developer. The only cases in which third parties were entitled to put forward their views, except for the 'administrative privilege' of appearing at public inquiries, were the so-called 'bad neighbour' developments – public conveniences, slaughter-houses, dance halls, and so on. Third parties could object to the planning application and, if it were *not* granted and went to inquiry, they could be heard there.

THE PRESENT SYSTEM

When the Planning Advisory Group reported in 1965, it claimed that the 1947 provisions were, at their enactment, the most advanced system of planning in the world. But experience and the intervening pattern of development had shown up weaknesses. Although much more effective than in the 1930s, planning was still insufficiently comprehensive to deal with such issues as the rapid increase in private transport or town centre redevelopment. A more strategic and creative system was required which would incorporate social and economic, as well as physical, factors. The general rights of objection needed to be given to third parties. The planning process needed to be speeded up. It had taken fourteen years for all authorities to submit their plans after 1947. There were long delays in dealing with planning applications and appeals.

The system presently operating, under the 1968 Town and Country Planning Act, was intended to remedy these defects. It provides for the preparation of structure plans and local (including action area) plans. The former are prepared by county authorities and are basically a statement of broad policies and proposals to cover an extended period of time. Structure plans do not include maps nor detailed land-use allocations. Within the framework of a structure plan, local plans are the responsibility of district councils. Local plans are more detailed, though the extent of detail can vary considerably. Unlike structure plans, they do not require the approval of the Secretary of State. Local matters have thus become a local responsibility to a greater degree than before, both politically and administratively. Any inquiry into a local plan will be held by an independent inspector who, unlike most other cases, will report to the local authority rather than to the Secretary of State.

The significance of some of these innovations has been pointed up by Cullingworth (1972: 305). 'The concept of ministerial responsibility has been shown to be inapplicable over the total field of development plan approval and appeals against planning decisions.' The centralisation of the post-war period turned out to be quite unwieldy. During the 1960s there was an annual average of more than 11,000 local planning inquiries, but in very few cases did the minister need to be involved in the decision. Attention to local issues was distracting the central administration from the task of helping government construct clear, national planning objectives. Cullingworth (1972: 308) states that 'the transfer of considerable statutory powers from central to local government will show only too clearly that planning is essentially a political process – a fact which has been confused by the semi-judicial procedures within which the Department [of the Environment] has been so preoccupied.' Both tiers of government had been encouraged to ignore the politics of planning. Local government saw its activities as regulated from the centre. The public also viewed planning primarily as a regulative matter. But now that the debate occurs entirely at a local level against a background of prior participation, the political nature of the issues should become apparent.

INVOLVEMENT THROUGH PUBLIC INQUIRIES

The semi-judicial nature of inquiries, which in the post-war period were the only formal avenue for involvement in the planning process, was only one source of complaint. A misunderstanding of the purpose and procedures of inquiries, the cynical view that government was acting as prosecutor, judge and jury, and the real difficulties which private individuals had in attending, let alone participating in, the proceedings were other causes of discontent. The time taken to hear an appeal and issue a decision, which has been estimated (Dobry 1975) to have been on average three times as long as was strictly necessary, seemed to characterise a grinding, bureaucratic machine, remote and inimical to the interests of citizens. The concentration on deciding matters of fact rather than value and the entirely discretionary role of those members of the public who had no legal interest in the land being developed were particular points of aggravation to the increasing number of amenity and other groups which were seeking to influence planning decisions.

But, in principle, the balance between private and public interest *had* shifted after 1947. The changes in policy over compensation had been one element. More important was the growing belief that the control of land development should be used to promote public purposes. In 1973 a Department of the Environment circular (DOE 1973a, para. 3) expressed the view that 'Planning is concerned to ensure that in the development of land the public interest is taken fully into account. Its objective is not the safe-guarding of private property rights as such; nor in particular, to protect the value of individual properties or the views to be had from them.' The notion that participation might be a matter for the public rather than for individual or sectional interests was referred to by Dobry (1975) in his *Review of the Development Control System*: he asked whether we are over-sensitive about protection of the rights of the individual in the conduct of inquiries.

The inquiry system in the early 1970s was in a parlous state. Apart from the public doubts already referred to, there were now more inquiries (over 17,000 in one year) than could be managed.

One of Dobry's tasks was to review the arrangements for appeals. Most of his comments and suggestions were administrative and tended in the direction of convenience for the two parties most immediately concerned, although it was recognised that third parties should have rights in the proceedings.

One section of the *Review* did deal with public involvement. It recognised that the public has expertise to offer to the planning process. The public wish, and should be encouraged, to contribute at an early stage. The knowledge possessed by amenity societies and their eagerness to become involved are particularly drawn attention to. The introduction of 'community land' by the 1975 Community Land Act (now repealed) required that someone should be strongly placed to oppose any local authority development which may be inappropriate. With the reorganisation of local government, elected members have a wider scope of interest and may not be able to supply as much detailed knowledge on local matters as the electorate. The latter two reasons of Dobry for public involvement have considerable implications for the balance of power in local government.

However, despite recognising these arguments and the complaints of the public towards the appeals system, Dobry has rather few improvements to suggest other than better communications. Apart from the greater involvement of third parties and the awarding of positive costs, the most far-reaching proposal would be to formalise earlier consultation and meetings, within the context of appeals. The inquiry machinery remains consultative rather than participatory. Doubts about the role of individuals and groups persist.

Members of the public make a valuable contribution to inquiries but some have little idea of what is relevant (Dobry 1975: 11.129). The contribution of the public to the appeal process must at the same time be both strongly encouraged and firmly constrained. This is more easily said than done. There is sometimes a difficulty in encouraging the general public to participate in even the most important inquiries, except where their private interests are directly affected. It is equally difficult to restrain a sincere but irrelevant objection of a local pressure group (Dobry 1975: 11.141).

We shall see that these comments can be applied to participation in planning more generally. Here they point up some of the problems of the inquiry system. Although inquiries were set up to inform central government of the facts of a case which was in doubt, the public had other aspirations for them. When participation was being encouraged elsewhere, it was not unreasonable for people to expect the scope of inquiries to be widened to include more fundamental issues and more interested parties. Those who wished to push forward participatory objectives have exploited the administrative shortcomings, particularly in the case of inquiries on trunk road proposals (Chapter 5). The appeals system was never intended to make participation possible. But its history and its persistence in a virtually unchanged form since 1968 has cast doubt for some on the integrity of participatory planning.

THE PLANNING PROFESSION

Public inquiries have been the most evident part of the planning process, if not of its products, for most of the population. Well before the trunk road furore of the 1970s, there was a series of well-publicised instances, such as those described in *The Price of Amenity* (Gregory 1971) – ironstone working, power stations, a North Sea gas terminal, the siting of a reservoir. They contributed to the image of planning as slow, contentious, bureaucratic and remote. The excesses of suburban sprawl and other uncontrolled development which outraged aesthetic sensibilities in the 1930s were considerably diminished after the war. But since then people began instead to be disturbed by the inadequacy of roads or of public transport and by the speed and extent of change to town centres. They became antagonistic towards planning decisions which they felt were not informed by the needs and aspirations of the public themselves.

The antagonism communicated itself to the planning profession. The Town Planning Institute (*Journal of the TPI* 1968) in its memorandum to the Skeffington Committee wrote: 'It is not surprising that planning is unpopular with many members of the public.' Professor Colin Buchanan, a leading member of the profession, even saw the antagonism as turned back upon itself. He is reported (Davies 1972: 95) as saying that the British character was in basic conflict with town and country planning, and that even the planners had 'joined a silent conspiracy not to make [planning legislation] work, because, deep down, we do not really approve of it.'

Some of the reasons for the unpopularity were drawn out in two case studies done in the late 1960s and early 1970s in Newcastle upon Tyne (Davies 1972) and Sunderland (Dennis 1970, 1972). For example, planners were portrayed as being driven by a revelatory vision of the 'New Jerusalem' which simultaneously excites self-esteem in themselves and hostility in others. Forward-looking policies attack established positions and create uncertainty which is the peculiar preserve of the planner. As Dennis (1972: 242) suggests:

... even those versions (of planning) which are relatively modest make large claims which tend to raise sights above any target which would require familiarity with the needs and feelings of ordinary consumers in the here and now .... The planner is freed from the present by his commitment to the future, and this scientificality can all be poured into anchorless data the validity of which cannot be checked.

The New Town movement is the prime example of the two forces at work. The purist ideals of Ebenezer Howard have been translated through the systematics of Geddes into a branch of high technology. All the apparatus of computers, systems analysts, urban networks, complex transportation modes, and so on were brought to bear in the 1960s on the planning of new and expanding towns. If the towns have been unpopular for other reasons, technological planning is still held to account. Values may be concealed by jargon and it is the jargon which is attacked.

The way in which post-war planning impinged on the concept of landed property inevitably drew a hostile response. Previously it had seemed to protect it. A very high proportion of the available wealth of all classes is rooted in property, which is frequently adversely affected by planning decisions. But it is not only a matter of selfish interest.

'The difficulty of measuring public gain against private loss, real or imagined, is accentuated in the case of planning by the very fact that to a considerable extent the public gain has to be taken on trust. It may not be capable of being proved for a generation or more whether some of the planning policies now being pursued have achieved what they were intended to achieve' (*Journal of the TPI* 1968).

But neither is it only a matter of property. The social goals of comprehensive planning can take in the whole of the citizen's life. What he may view as interference will touch not only on his home and housing conditions, but on his employment, mobility, recreational opportunities, educational and health provision and so on. The interference is carried through by an apparently bureaucratic body which rules by statutory powers and sanctions, which must regulate in order to promote.

Many of the citizen's doubts touch on characteristics of the planning profession itself rather than on its sphere of activity. The doubts equally haunt the profession, and even go to inform the professional identity. Davies (1972: 95) observes that '... it is this sense of being perpetually embattled, misunderstood and unpopular which is responsible for the peculiar intensity of the planner's claim to professional status'. The battle is not just with the public. Comprehensive planning invades other professions. The reaction of government departments to the inclusion, as topics in structure plans, of education, social services and housing, for example, was determined and successful. And yet these same professions are demanding that planners be increasingly accountable for the details of their proposals' effects.

The planner's heavy reliance on statutory powers makes him unlike other professionals who are legitimised through a specific expertise and a well-established ethical code. The overlap of planning with architecture, sociology, engineering, agriculture and so on has made some wonder whether there is such a thing as planning. It is perhaps to compensate for these characteristics of the profession that planning problems tend simultaneously to be defined in a highly technical fashion and to be informed by all-encompassing, millennial values. But it is then precisely the conjunction of two apparently unassailable positions that becomes so infuriating to the lay person.

The responsibility wielded by the planner in local government has been objected to on political grounds. When the advice he gives to the elected decision-maker is complex, technical and detailed, it is dubious who makes the decisions. Many planning committees have effectively allowed their officers to govern policy and take decisions because they themselves are unable to comprehend the technicalities, master the enormous workload potential, or even grasp the political implications of planning. The balance of power between the professions and local government must be interpreted in the light of the following factors: planners control certain forms of knowledge; they control the form of reports to committees and to council; they implement decisions; and in practice, they monitor the efficiency of planning policies and proposals. Against this form of practice, on fundamental issues, for example, of resource distribution between different socioeconomic classes, the planner's claim to be apolitical is a shaky proposition.

The public may be largely unaware of the way in which it is governed until it confronts an authority with a problem. When that happens the anomalous relation between public, officers and members cannot be concealed. The anomaly may or may not be removed by the discretionary delegation to officers of many planning application decisions, which authorities are empowered to make under the 1968 Act. There is no need to feel that the decisions will become more remote from the public with this arrangement: we know that citizens have as much, if not more, contact with officers as with councillors. Delegating these decisions to officers may leave the elected members more time for political debate of policy issues. But the possible implication that development control can then be treated as an apolitical matter strikes at the heart of planning's position in local democratic government.

The ambiguous nature of the planning profession and its relations with the public and with politicians has produced an equal confusion of motives for promoting participation. The technical face of planning may believe that it will lead to a greater chance of plans being implemented and therefore to more effective planning. The 'embattled' planner hopes that it will bring better relations with the general public, removing some of the grounds for hostility. In local government, it may bring a path to legitimation which runs directly from the electorate, rather than uncertainly through the elected member. Even social goals may be served by participation if these are identified in terms of the values which the public itself promotes.

STRUCTURE PLANS

Ideally the enactment in 1968 of wider public involvement than hitherto should have been an occasion for encouraging both the public and local authorities that it was a viable and fruitful measure. Before 1968 the major form of involvement, public inquiries, had been highly restricted and productive of frustration and resentment on all sides. Many of the earliest opportunities for public involvement in planning under the 1968 Act occurred in the structure plan process. Because a structure plan dealt with matters of broad policy, its preparation has generally preceded the detailed elaboration of proposals in a local plan, which has anyway to conform to the structure plan.

Structure planning was certainly a quite different arena for involvement than planning applications and appeals. Its geographical focus was often as deep as the extent of a medium-sized county. Detailed land-use allocations were not included. Policies were to deal with a range of social and economic conditions and were based on reports of survey of such topics as population, employment, transport and housing. The plan's written statement and 'key diagram' (but no map) was therefore likely to be a complex and abstract document. A broad stretch of time as well as of territory was covered by the plan: initially this was envisaged as a twenty-year period. The problems entailed by attempting to plan for such a lengthy period led to a concept of structure planning as a continuing activity. Continual monitoring and re-surveying were intended to make the structure plan an evolving or malleable process rather than having the appearance of a final product as did the previous generation of development plans.

On the face of it these characteristics made structure plans even less inviting to the public than planning appeals and inquiries. They also promised to accentuate the roles of the technocratic, visionary, and comprehensive planner which had already created hostility between the public and the profession. Difficulties of understanding were as likely to afflict the elected members, who in most cases had no more time or expertise than the lay person to fathom the lengthy and complex documents.

The function and content of structure plans was puzzling to the public. Abstract, strategic policies projecting as much as a generation ahead were an unfamiliar notion to people whose everyday plans and decisions were by comparison, immediate, short term and concrete. Lives tend to be so static that long-term planning of them is irrelevant, or so mobile that five or six years would be the very furthest forseeable horizon. Geographically, people were often well-travelled, if they had private transport. But even if they had covered more than a small proportion of the structure plan area they would be unlikely to be interested in or sympathetic towards planning problems that lay ten or more miles away from home. And yet the systemic nature of structure planning demanded that they appreciate *overall* strategies of settlement pattern, transportation networks, and shopping and other service hierarchies. Although such broadly based planning, over the area of as many as two dozen of the pre-1974 local authorities, promised to solve many of the historical problems of the planning process, they were not likely to draw in an interested public.

The programme typically adopted for preparing a structure plan and going to the public produced difficulties. If the first documents presented to the public were reports of survey, they were likely to be misunderstood as being planning proposals or found excessively dry and technical with little in them to excite comment. In other cases people were asked to identify the major problems in the area in which they lived, to say which issues their plan should be tackling. But if they responded, they might have to wait for several years before they saw the outcome of their suggestions in a written plan document. Such an extended planning process is liable to lead to cynicism on the part of those who do try to participate if they have to wait a long time for feedback on their efforts. It will inevitably frustrate attempts to apply Skeffington's precept of involvement in the formulation of policies and proposals at an early formative stage. The time-scales of the structure plan process and of its goals are both out of phase with that of everyday life.

The public affected by a structure plan has always been very large, upward of half-a-million people. The term 'public participation' may have suggested that everyone should have been invited to participate, however improbable that now seems. Despite Skeffington's reference to the heterogeneity of the public, it has frequently been addressed as a single mass audience with common understanding, aspirations and expectations. As a result particular sectional or geographical interests have been missed which by a more differentiated approach could have been readily enabled to participate. Planners have been disappointed by the numbers which they reached because, however large in absolute terms, they have always been a small proportion of the total population which the planners believed should be engaged. Defining the public as a collectivity, an aggregate set of individuals each of whom should receive a pamphlet through the letter-box or be randomly sampled to answer a questionnaire, goes against the philosophy of planning which promotes the public good rather than individual interests. A strategy for participation consistent with this philosophy would work at a level beyond that of the individual.

A number of planning authorities recognised this and operated a form of pluralism. The emphasis in participation was within groups and organisations, either as representing particular interests or as convenient channels for the wider communication of information from and to the authority. But the problems of pluralism at the scale of national democratic systems were also present at the structure plan level. Some people cannot be identified with a group at all easily. Others may belong to a number of groups simultaneously. This can lead sometimes to a conflict of loyalties in the individual; and to the possibility of over-representation of those sectional interests which coincide with overlapping group membership. There is a very large number of groups which might potentially make a contribution. Many are difficult to identify or locate, or, despite the assumptions of pluralism, do not see it as their business to act as a group in response to planning proposals. There is considerable variation between groups, country-wide, in the extent of their expertise. The skills of experienced consultees have often been respected by planners, but the tactics of practised pressure groups have not been. Individual representations on planning proposals are always assumed to be unrepresentative, and group representations are often suspected of being so.

The wording of the 1968 Act appeared to set limited objectives for public involvement. There was to be 'adequate publicity' and an opportunity to comment for those 'who might be expected to wish to do so'. Obtaining a response from the public was an incidental benefit to be derived from publicity rather than the goal to be achieved. Provided that the authority could ascertain who might reasonably wish to comment on a structure plan and gave them the opportunity to do so, its statutory obligations seemed to be satisfied. Research studies of structure plan participation (Boaden *et al.* 1980) have shown that much greater efforts have been made to inform the public that a plan was being prepared and what the major issues were, than to develop a responsive public. But even information-giving has rarely promoted more than a public awareness. To enable people to comprehend such complex issues and to evaluate alternative proposals requires communication skills which have not yet been fostered by the planner's training.

At the structure plan level a great deal of the attention given by officers to participation focused on 'techniques', particularly techniques for information dissemination. The problems of participation were assumed to be technical – what media to use – rather than strategic. Objectives were rarely discussed, the audience was assumed and the outcome was scarcely evaluated. But given the unlikely nature of structure planning as a vehicle for wide participation, the attention was even more misdirected – vastly improved techniques could bring only very small increases in participation.

The techniques chosen were usually those which are under a local authority's control. But their corresponding disadvantage is that they are mostly unfamiliar to the potential audience. Everyone knows what an exhibition or public meeting is, but it is rarely a resource which people know how to use for their own purposes. They can only approach it on the terms laid down by its organisers. If 'planners' media' must be used, they should be sensitive to the details of everyday life. There are times of the year, of the week, of the evening, and there are particular locations which are inviting to an audience; others which will keep it at bay.

Sensitivity to the other's point of view can be recommended for the public as well as for local government. But the latter is potentially the more tractable body. It alone has the statutory duty to engage in participation. But sensitivity is probably not the major issue in achieving a 'client-centred' approach. The larger obstacle is the concept of professional responsibility within a framework of nominal accountability. It is this which places superordinate importance on the inviolability of the plan drawn up by the professionals. While the goal is to maintain its inviolability, to deny lay people access to the actual business of planning, it is unlikely that the asymmetry of much current participation will be rectified. It is not necessary in this argument to conceive of participation as direct involvement in decision-making. Even where participation is interpreted simply in terms of improved communications, it cannot effectively be achieved in a one-way system.

The scale at which structure plans operate has produced considerable problems when the public has responded. A county planning department might offer to visit and speak to interested organisations and be overwhelmed if more than a few dozen accept. Pre-paid leaflet-questionnaires are usually returned in their hundreds: an authority which receives, say, 10,000 completed forms, albeit still from a minority of the population, is unlikely to have the manpower to process them. Even modest numbers of written representations can be very time-consuming to analyse and to reply to. To anticipate these problems a number of structure plan authorities carried out random sample surveys of the electorate at one or other stage of the plan preparation programme. A survey guarantees the number of respondents and their representativeness. The information which needs to be collected is determined in advance by the planning department. Its coding and analysis can be carried out according to a formal scheme and at a known cost.

In practice, however, the advantages of a sample survey are not so apparent. It is doubtful whether the information gathered can be termed a 'participatory response' from the public. Only a few people are actually allowed to participate in this way. The terms of reference are firmly set by the other party. Survey questions are usually asked in a vacuum without the input of supporting information and with little indication of how answers will be treated or what the implications of particular answers may be.

The survey tends to 'individualise' people's involvement in the planning process. They are treated as units. It offers little scope for tapping values and intentions in the social context in which they are formulated and have their meaning. Respondents are usually individuals speaking for themselves rather than families or groupings with common interests, centred, for example, on the street or workplace. This tendency is aggravated if results are not thoroughly disaggregated to reveal grouped responses from those sectional and areal categories which are represented in the survey sample. A danger of the survey is that it may reduce participation to the form of the referendum.

Whether or not a sample survey is consistent with the notion of participation, there has not yet been a demonstration that its results can be used effectively. Even if the right questions have been asked and a comprehensive analysis conducted, structure plan teams do not seem to have been able to incorporate the information into their suggested policies and proposals. Usually the survey questionnaires have had a strong attitudinal and evaluative component. But the 'technology' of attitude and value measurement is of a different order from the technologies which planners use. Technical means for integrating quantitative and qualitative information are wanting; the qualitative is left to one side. In a few cases planners have assumed that the results of attitude surveys, but not by implication of other types of survey, are political material. They have been handed to elected members to help them make the final decisions as to which policies and proposals to adopt.

Participation in planning to date has tended to be planner orientated. The planning department has usually been the body to initiate a local plan process, to conduct surveys and draw up alternatives. Members of this department compose the publicity to announce their proposals and disseminate it through channels over which they have control, and at times which are convenient to their programme. Understandably they do this in the hope of improving their planning process; they are not prepared for a complete rebuttal of their proposals or lengthy negotiations for modified plans. As professionals they cannot accept reinterpretations of their plans nor plans drawn up by unqualified people.

Whether or not participation has improved the planning process, as far as planners are concerned, is open to question. There is not much evidence of 'better plans'; and it has been claimed that participation adds to the time and cost of the process. But a number of planners seem sincere in welcoming opportunities for greater contact with the public and for thinking more about their objectives for participation. As far as the public is concerned, small gains have probably been achieved, for some sectors at least, through structure plan participation: primarily in any increased awareness of the planning process rather than by an definitive input to it. Provided that the frustration of unrealistic expectations on the part of planners and public has not bred cynicism, the first efforts at statutory participation will have been worth while for both parties.

But what of the third party, the administrators? The administrators' motives for participation should be fairly clear in the light of our earlier discussion. The Secretary of State retains central control of the structure plan process, by having the plans submitted for his approval. At the same time a door of appeal to him is to be left open for any interested parties, and the opportunity is expected as a rule to be used. What is to be avoided, however, is a repetition of the Greater London Development Plan Inquiry which drew forth more than 20,000 objections and lasted for more than a year. Inquiries on that scale are very expensive, and they retard the planning process. (Though one wonders what constitutes a significant delay in a system where less than two-thirds of structure plans had been submitted ten years after the 1968 Act.) They bring up issues of fact and opinion which could have been elicited much earlier. Above all, for the administrator, they are unduly public and contentious. The administrative rationale for participation is to anticipate as far as possible the two principal aims of inquiries – to gather relevant factual information from the public and to give an opportunity for open debate on the issues involved in a planning proposal. If participation is effective these two goals will have been largely achieved before an inquiry.

In the arrangements made for considering objections to a structure plan – the 'Examination in Public' – it is assumed to a large extent that the goals have been reached. The Secretary of State has a statutory duty to consider all objections. However, for the Examination in Public he is now exercising his right to determine who should be permitted to take part. Only selected matters are discussed, by selected authorities, organisations and individuals. The potentially adversarial nature of inquiries is glossed over. The Examination is not for the purpose of hearing objections. 'The traditional form of inquiry, which has come to involve many formalities of a kind apt for dealing with detailed property matters, has only rarely proved suitable for exploring also the policy issues inherent in major development plan submissions' (DOE 1973c: 4). However, it is not clear that the Examination has made such explorations possible. Debates of policy questions between the local authorities and the public have been overshadowed by technical discussions of the feasibility and implementation of a plan between local authorities, public bodies and commercial interests. In practice, the Examination in Public has assumed that policy issues have been adequately debated during structure plan preparation. It is unfortunate that no institutionalised measures have been established that would facilitate adequacy of debate as well as of publicity over planning proposals.

Statutory participation in planning, which has been the subject of this chapter, is of course not limited to structure planning. However, the most concentrated and commented on experience to date has been at that level. Planning authorities have been slow to begin work on statutory local plans under the new legislation. Moreover, structure plan participation has been more extensively researched than the small-scale, brief and scattered instances of local plan participation. Even if many of the general principles raised are probably at issue at all levels of planning, structure plans provide a quite particular context for participation. It is convenient to leave reference to local plan participation, which has most often in practice been of a non-statutory form, until the two following chapters.

Chapter five

TRANSPORTATION

During the 1960s and 1970s the most noticeable grass-roots demands for participation in policy-making and implementation, or perhaps the loudest protests against policy decisions, occurred when the physical environment was threatened with change. People's surroundings quickly become familiar to them and in the process offer identity and security. The permanence and immobility of the existing environment is a comfort, particularly in times of other rapid change. Paradoxically, the permanence promised by a new environment is seen as a threat.

In the post-war period the consciousness of change has been continually sharpened. Technological developments and relative affluence have made gross environmental changes possible and desirable. Many of them have centred on housing, transport and recreation. Home ownership and better housing standards, mobility and an active use of increased leisure time were valued and enjoyed more than ever before. But the benefits had their disadvantages. Slum clearance, for example, destroyed long-established communities. More cars produced congested town centres or urban motorways to relieve them. Large-scale developments in industry, housing and the road network led to noisy, polluted, unaesthetic surroundings. They were met by protest groups – tenants' associations, groups against the motorway, and conservationists. Ironically, apart from the commercial road lobby, those who wanted the developments and would benefit from them did not raise their voices. Implicitly they allowed the policy-makers to speak for them. The debate was one between government and the protesters.

The main interest here, however, is not in these groups themselves. In this and the following chapter we are examining the opportunities which government has allowed to the public more generally to participate in the provision of transportation and hous-

Transportation

ing. A part, but not all of government's motives for participation was to contain and counter-balance pressure groups.

If trunk road planning dominated the public attention in the 1970s, it was largely because of a spate of contentious and uproarious inquiries. New roads aroused more objections than disappearing public transport services. But the imbalance was pushed further by government's tendency to treat these two arms of transport separately. Subsequent to the 1930 Road Traffic Act there have been a number of further enactments dealing with public transport. Road policy, on the other hand, has until very recently been little more than a series of assumptions – acted on by civil servants, but rarely debated. The separation is strengthened by the fact that, by common law and statute, road provision is at the public expense rather than for profit.

In the post-war period the development plans which were produced by local authorities included limited proposals for road improvements. During the 1950s a programme of inter-urban motorways and highway improvements was introduced and increasing attention was given to traffic problems in urban areas. Despite, or perhaps because of, a rapid growth in car ownership, unrestricted use of the car was assumed to be a reasonable planning objective. By the mid-1960s road construction and improvement figured largely in development plan reviews. The number of registered vehicles on the roads rose from 9.5 millions in 1960 to 14.9 millions ten years later. While in the preceding decade the number of new car registrations had risen from 132,000 to 805,000 per year. Although many county boroughs proposed ambitious schemes, with large radial roads and inner city ring roads, there was little public reaction at this stage. Transport planning had become, and was presented as, a highly technical exercise: relying on distant projections of car ownership and population figures and on complex quantification of 'trip generation', 'trip distribution', 'modal split' and 'traffic assignment'.

By 1972 there were 1,600 principal road schemes lodged for approval by the Department of the Environment – many of them representing hurried attempts to finalise plans before the reorganisation of local government. More recently highway construction has been cut back on several occasions, due to fuel crises or economic recession. But car ownership increases still – although not at the rate predicted previously – encouraged by a spiralling urban dispersal and deterioration in public transport services. Individual mobility is assumed to be necessarily beneficial to all who can afford it, despite its negative feedback on levels of public transport provision for those who cannot.

The Road Traffic Act of 1930 introduced legislation to public transport, by requiring buses and coaches to be licensed by regional Traffic Commissioners. They also supervised the details of routes, timetables and fares; and considered the provision of unremunerative services and the co-ordination of services. The Act abolished the chaotic competition between operators which had sometimes existed previously, but it led instead to the establishment of large, semi-monopolistic concerns. An element of participation can be found at this early date. Any party who was affected by proposals put before the Traffic Commissioners could object and a public meeting would be held to hear the objection. In practice, however, this opportunity was not widely used.

The 1968 Transport Act is generally taken as a watershed in transportation planning. It was motivated by a wish to rationalise the transport industry. Economy was to be achieved by mergers, especially of small municipal undertakings. Grants from central government were to be made available to certain elements of public transport. In conurbations Public Transport Authorities and Public Transport Executives were set up in order to produce a transportation network which integrated all services. The PTAs and PTEs had much wider powers and duties than the undertakings which they replaced. But although a general policy had to be published, there was no encouragement of public involvement in their activity.

TRANSPORT POLICIES AND PROGRAMMES

A measure of integration of road with public transport planning might have been expected with the introduction in 1974 of Transport Policies and Programmes (TPPs). These statements were to be produced by all counties annually. Their proposals should fall within the framework of the structure plan and include policies for the next ten to fifteen years and a five-year rolling programme. This non-statutory system was intended to reduce central government's involvement in local policy on a project-by-project basis, by introducing block grants for a five-year rolling programme. The virtue is that there is greater local flexibility and accountability. Much of the advantage, however, is taken away by loan sanction arrangements. The borrowing by local authorities of money for capital schemes costing more than £0.5 million has to be sanctioned by Whitehall after careful scrutiny. Just as the housing cost yardstick and the ever changing intricacies of housing finance deprive councillors of much effective control over their local housing situation, so too in transport matters priorities and co-ordinated schemes have been difficult to establish. There is a temptation to boost the number of loan sanction applications in the hope that at least some will come through. To think of the public being deeply involved in policy-making of this kind is ambitious indeed.

The financial emphasis in TPPs was sufficient to persuade the Chartered Institute of Public Finance and Accountancy to produce a special report on them (CIPF 1976). Its authors had several criticisms, apart from purely financial ones. For example, they believed that the system was too complex and cumbersome for elected members to understand. They drew attention to the multiplicity of relationships which consultation on TPPs entailed: with transport operators, other policy-makers (such as neighbouring counties), pressure groups and the general public. Because local authority boundaries do not coincide with transport requirements, the sheer number of interauthority negotiations may be too much of a burden. District councils have complained of having insufficient time to comment on TPPs. And yet they may have delegated responsibilities for some roads and bus services. They are responsible for car-parking and detailed land-use planning. Metropolitan districts have education and social services departments, as well as housing – all of which functions relate to transport provision.

The fact that TPPs are prepared on a continuous annual cycle, with interdepartmental and interauthority consultation and a decision coming from the Minister four or five months after submission, scarcely leaves time for much public participation. None has been urged in DOE/DTp circulars, and little has occurred. It is relatively easy for specific issues, such as lorry routes, to be debated in public, provided that their relationship to the overall programme can be explained. Otherwise the discussion of general policy is complicated by the uncertain relations between TPPs and structure plans. Early difficulties over their integration were compounded by the renewed separation in 1976 of the Department of Transport from the Department of the Environment.

ROAD PLANNING

Transportation was open to public discussion during the 1970s as a topic in the preparation of structure plans. But we have suggested that such discussion was not very extensive. A more promising context is the preparation of local plans which contain some transportation implications. Though, because of their differing responsibilities, some co-operation between county and district councils is required if that is to be successful. The former are highway authorities (except for trunk roads and motorways, which are a central government responsibility); while the districts look after local land-use issues and car-parking. They may act as an agency for the county council for maintaining and improving roads, but this is not always the case.

A recent example in which co-operation did occur was at Saxmundham in Suffolk (Aldous 1980). A joint exercise in participation was mounted by the two authorities over plans to build a bypass and to cater for growth in the town. They prepared an explanatory booklet, and a leaflet summary of it was posted through all letter boxes. It included a questionnaire. People were asked to send their answers to the district council, to avoid confusion between the authorities. A week-long exhibition was held in a vacant shop. The presentation had maps, photo-montages and a tape-slide show. An officer from each authority visited every property affected by any of the three bypass options to explain and discuss the proposals. In the event the exercise produced a 40 per cent response from the public – far in excess of that which had been received in a similar exercise three years previously. The officers felt that they had learned few new facts as a result of the public's response; but they had gained a greater awareness of how people thought the proposals would affect them in practice – for example, by severance.

The ingredients of this exercise are not altogether atypical, but it did have some unusual features. The authorities had learnt from their previous experience: they took more time and care, and worked on a particularly attractive presentation. The tape-slide show probably contributed to this. The combination of issues – bypass and economic growth – interested people. Perhaps most important was the personal contact with the public which the officers achieved, and the way in which they interpreted it.

Although the residents of Saxmundham got the plan which the majority of them preferred, there were several weak points in the exercise. It tended, for example, to individualise the public's response. Questionnaires were delivered to households; they may or may not have been read and completed by just one person. No public meeting or similar forum seems to have been organised by the authorities which would have enabled people to become aware of their collective interests. Although the questionnaire was not intended as a poll or head-count, it may have been seen in that light. Another weakness was that the exercise ultimately was concerned with the authorities' interests. The officers are on record as being encouraged by people's logical and fair-minded responses. They opted for the planners' preferred proposal. What would have been the benefit of the exercise for the public if the officials had decided otherwise? There should be a benefit in participation as such. But virtually all the available reports of participation exercises are written from the authority's perspective and neglect this point.

A combination of issues has also been presented to the public in participation on General Improvement Areas (GIAs) (DOE 1973b). They were intended as a means of both environmental and house improvement. The 1963 Buchanan Report introduced the notion of environmental areas, anticipating the GIA legislation by several years. They were to be free of extraneous traffic, and environmental considerations would predominate over the use of vehicles. Many GIAs have effected a great part of their improvements by excluding through traffic, whether by restriction or road closure and pedestrianisation. Provision is also made wherever possible for off-street parking.

Schemes of this kind reduce the noise level, pollution, congestion and danger to pedestrians in urban streets. The street becomes a more livable and healthy environment, a neighbourly territory, a place for play. Hopefully community identity becomes more secure both physically and through participation in a local scheme. Area improvement involves personal sacrifices as well as gains – one of the main lessons of participation in service provision generally. It may be necessary for householders to provide off-street parking themselves or to give up a part of their garden for wider pavements, rear access lanes or some other amenity. They may no longer be able to park directly outside their house. But where there is participation and discussion between the community and the authority these losses can be borne by individuals.

A more difficult issue is the loss incurred by those who live near a GIA. Restraining traffic in one place usually redistributes it. In some cases this has led to violent opposition and conflict between neighbouring groups of streets. It may be possible to adopt an areal approach to smoke control or conservation, but other problems cannot be so easily contained. The local plan which a district council might prepare could provide an opportunity for competing claims to be debated. Unfortunately the elements of area policy were laid on to authorities before they were in a position to proceed with the preparation of local plans.

THE ROAD LOBBY AND GROUP OPPOSITION

We suggested above that the activities of pressure groups have been one of the most conspicuous aspects of the reactions to road proposals. This has been the case no matter what the scale of the proposals. The question we have to address here is whether such activities fall within the scope of public participation. Certainly the attitude of central and local government has been sceptical on this point. Their main concern has been over the possible unrepresentative nature of anti-road group opinion.

This concern, however, lies against a background of deep governmental involvement with the pro-road lobby (Hamer 1974: 57).

The road lobby is the strongest and most politically active pressure group seeking to shape the future of this country. Its understanding of the mechanics of the political process at both national and local levels is unparalleled amongst lobbying groups. The scope and depth of its ambitions make it almost unique amongst non-governmental bodies. Its resources, both actual and potential make it almost impossible for any opposing group to match the extent of its efforts to get its voice heard . . . there is one voice that is heard more than any opposing voice and . . . this voice has a position of privilege.

Railways and waterways have no comparable champion. The major areas of support for the road lobby are the motor industry, bus operators, road haulage firms, motorists' organisations, and the road construction and oil industries. Indirectly it can claim to represent considerable economic and social interests. It shuns publicity and had a close working relationship with government. Unlike the environmental groups which have opposed juggernauts or the road building programme, it is strongly organised and co-ordinated at a national level.

Despite the proliferation of environmental or amenity groups in recent years (the number of those registered with the Civic Trust rose from a handful in 1957 to more than 1,250 in 1976), they often have a number of features not shared by the road lobby, which prevent them from being effective channels for participation (Kimber and Richardson 1974). They lack advance information about authorities' proposals and so are forced into a rearguard action of opposition against heavy time odds. The resources and expertise which are required to put forward a convincing argument against what are represented as purely technical proposals are generally not available to local groups. Unless they are particularly sophisticated, they are unlikely to appreciate the need for a close and continuing liaison with the authorities or to include officers and councillors on their committees.

Ironically, if groups do have the motivation and skills required they are likely to be seen as unrepresentative. Their talents will be due to a predominantly middle class and professional membership. Often they will be found to be fighting for an amenity which they enjoy, in a situation where their victory would entail a loss to a less privileged sector of the community. Road planners have found great difficulty in incorporating amenity into their equations. It introduces a political element into what they prefer to be purely rational and technical considerations. The groups themselves are also reluctant to recognise that their interests are political. By yielding to the pressure which exists in the consultative process itself, to concentrate on the narrow, localised impact of environmental change, they lose sight of the broader issues of policy which are inescapably political.

The problem with pressure groups is not that they are unrepresentative of public opinion – in one sense they are bound to be; but that theirs is usually a privileged voice. The authority's task then has to be to identify and weigh other viewpoints which are not so openly expressed. The community development officer proposed by the Skeffington Committee is one mechanism by which people might be helped to articulate their views. But in the face of government opposition to the idea, planners have more usually resorted to sample surveys of individual preferences. As we point out elsewhere, poll-taking is an exceptionally weak form of participation which does nothing to help people appreciate their collective interests. It has been found in several case studies of road proposal consultations (SCPR 1975) that a sample survey may almost exactly reproduce the opinions put forward by the very small minority who actually respond to a consultation exercise. But even if that correspondence could be guaranteed in every case, neither the people sampled nor the majority who do not respond to consultation can be said to have participated, even indirectly.

MOTORWAYS AND TRUNK ROADS

The most visible sign of public involvement in transportation issues has been over motorways and trunk roads. It was fuelled in the early 1970s by increasing environmental concern, a scepticism about the wisdom of 'experts', and an end to the consensus that new roads are necessarily a good thing. The publication, for example, of the Greater London Development Plan (GLDP) in 1969 brought the matter to one of several climaxes of the past decade. (Other notable cases occurred at Epping, the Aire Valley, Winchester and Archway.) The most important part of the GLDP was the proposal for a comprehensive web of motorways – four ringways and twelve radial routes. 'Homes before cars' became a catchphrase, and the subsequent public inquiry lasted a record length of time. Ringway is an example (Hart 1976) of a planning proposal in which community concerns were generally ignored, yet which was eventually overturned by the democratic concerns of the ballot box. When Labour regained the Greater London Council in April 1973 it followed its manifesto and scrapped the scheme.

A swing from Conservative to Labour has been observed (Grant 1977) in several other cities as presaging the death of ambitious road schemes, even though transport policy was incidental to the election. In three case-studies several other factors were also found to be necessary, though not sufficient, for a change in transport policy. They included the death, resignation or retirement of the City Engineer; the existence of a variety of anti-road groups; the size of the scheme; and at least one instance of the planners having been previously 'defeated' in a public inquiry. The most important point is that these factors involved all three principal actors in participation: the technicians (planners), the politicians, and the community. The demise of urban road schemes did not rest on the actions or characteristics of one party alone.

Although since 1973 provision has been made for consultation on trunk road proposals, two of the features surrounding the Ringway plan still dominate. We shall return to the question of public inquiries, which particularly during 1973–77 gained such notoriety, after discussing the relation between relevant authorities and its implication for participation.

The GLDP is an extreme example of complex relations. The Greater London Council had to contend with three departments in Whitehall (the Ministries of Transport, of Housing and Local Government, and the Treasury), with the thirty-two London boroughs, and with British Rail and London Transport. If there had been any desire for participation, the public's place in this web would have been ambiguous.

Most commonly public participation now occurs at the stage at which the alternative road alignments for a stretch of motorway are published. Information about the advantages and disadvantages of each route are given – such as the length, cost, traffic benefits, properties lost, landscape intrusion. Only alternatives which are judged to be feasible are published. If one is favoured by the planners, a statement is made to that effect. The government department, through the Road Construction Unit, publishes a document explaining the proposals, which includes a reply-paid questionnaire; and mounts an exhibition. A period of participation is set, of not less than six weeks.

These procedures, which were introduced in 1973, involve people at an earlier stage of the planning process than before. By allowing them to consider alternatives it was hoped that all-out opposition and confrontation at public inquiry would be avoided. Making a comparison between alternatives should give lay people some insight into the kind of process in which planners engage and allow them to make a more informed evaluation.

In practice, more information certainly has been given than before, and earlier; and people have had an opportunity to comment on available alternatives. But there have also been problems. Sometimes only partial or overly summary information has been given, and there has been an assumption that the public would and should accept the validity of 'technical data'. The period allowed for participation is often too short, particularly when it falls in the summer months or when, for example, groups wish to affiliate or to coordinate their representation. However well intentioned, the publication of alternative routes can lead to a blighting of property on all of them; in some cases a ministerial decision may be delayed for several years.

Most serious is the possibility for confusion over responsibilities. The need for the road is not open to discussion at this stage. It is assumed to have been decided by central government – though in practice this may well be a decision by civil servants rather than by elected members. The county is the highway authority, with statutory responsibility for public participation in structure planning and consequently with a duty to involve the public in plans for local roads, some of which will be determined by the trunk road. It may look as if participation is being invited on matters which have already been decided.

The county authority is in a spurious position when it is asked to collect and report local views to the Department of Transport through its Road Construction Unit (RCU). These units were set up by Whitehall to be responsible for the design and construction of trunk roads, but as many as 90 per cent of their staff are seconded from county authorities. The county may thus seem to be independently representing its electorate's opinion to an arm of central government, whilst in fact supplying the muscles and skeleton to that arm.

The county's and the RCU's position becomes even more complicated when planning work is sub-contracted to consulting engineers. This is not uncommon. But since they are engaged to carry out work preceding the planning stage at which participation normally occurs, involvement of the public is relatively unusual. One example when it did happen was an exercise undertaken a few years ago in Leicester (Mynors and Moore 1978). Consultants had been asked to investigate the evidence of need and possible routes for a bypass of Leicester. They set out to obtain views, opinions and information from the public on the need for a new road. They also devoted time to explaining the independent advisory role of consultants and their method of working. This exercise was in addition to the normal participation which would occur a year or two later when alternative route proposals might be published. At the time of writing a new complication in this relation has emerged. RCUs are to be phased out and the majority of the design and supervision of the motorway and trunk road programme is to be handed over to private enterprise.

If participation is to occur early in the decision-making cycle, and experts external to government are doing the major work at that stage, it seems logical that they approach the public. A parallel in the case of housing would be for a private architectural office to engage tenants in the design of a new housing scheme. There are disadvantages, however. The time factor is one, and this applies to any form of early participation. Even a housing scheme can take ten years to complete from its inception. Those who see the finished product may not have been available to participate at an earlier stage. Another difficulty is the danger of political misunderstanding when consultants are involved. They may appear to be gaining public legitimisation for the proposals or advice which they pass on to a local authority. If their recommendations are subsequently rejected, and their advisory role is not understood by the public, the authority is liable to be accused of bad faith. It may even feel under pressure to accept recommendations for that reason. The more agencies or levels of decision-making involved, the greater this danger is likely to be.

District councils also may experience some conflict in being asked simultaneously to comment themselves and to collect local opinion. They are well placed to mediate between the local interests which they represent and the sub-regional priorities given in the structure plan which they have to conform to. But their responsibility for organising participation on roads which are not their direct concern is highly discretionary and not often taken up. They are probably in an easier position to do so when the responsible authority is at the national rather than county or regional level. In cases of outstanding controversy, for example the siting of the third London airport, one finds district or county councils actively collaborating with the public in opposition to proposals. But more generally they can be forgiven for thinking that effective participation should be between the public and those who actually take the decisions.

Parish councils, on the other hand, have tended to be more active. They are more accustomed to consultation and discussion than to executive responsibilities. They are able to accept a mandate to represent a purely local point of view. In most cases a trunk road alignment which goes through the parish will damage its interests on a fairly large scale. Sometimes detailed local knowledge about, for example, soil conditions can be brought to bear.

In practice, parish councils have been energetic respondents to road planning participation (Stringer 1981). They have commented more frequently than other non-governmental local organisations which have been consulted; and have taken greater pains to elicit their electorate's views and integrate them into a coherent and representative statement. Public meetings and surveys have been used for this purpose fairly regularly. There is evidence that parish councils can act as an effective two-way channel of communication between higher tiers of government and the public.

At the same time their position in this relation is not altogether clear. In one case-study (Thornton and Stringer 1979), the motives of inactive parish councils are instructive. Several were uncertain as to whether they were to represent the electorate or should canvass public opinion. Another anticipated problem was in reflecting the public's view which consisted solely of opposition to the alternative route which affected it. A third reason for inactivity was the belief that little notice would be taken of views restricted to a small parish. Sections of the parish electorate would like the council to exercise a 'watch-dog' function and to adopt a campaigning approach. Although instances of this can be found, the councils seem more generally to prefer a stance which is indicative of incorporation into the governmental machinery.

The highly localised nature of parish councils and of the objections to a road scheme raises a question which is central to participation on proposals which are local in their negative impact, but highly ramified in their assumed benefits. We have already commented that local groups often wish to debate matters which have been previously decided at a strategic level. The paradox is that, while participation appears to be most feasible and more obviously effective at a local level, many choices have to be made on a broader geographical front. Transportation is the prime instance because it is our means of 'displacement', of getting away from or passing through the locality. With a few exceptions local interests are necessarily antagonistic to those of the traveller.

Parish, district and county councils have a different territory and a different perspective; and participation will be a different matter according to the level at which the public engages. Owner-occupiers in a settled middle-class commuter village have everything to lose, and the parish may well fight accordingly against the alternative route which impinges. The district may see certain benefits accruing for its immediate area. The district council is unlikely to know how to orchestrate an open debate between alternative routes and interests. In the absence of strong political considerations it may opt for an alternative which will further the authority's advantage: a line which will use a long-demolished and embarrassing clearance area, for example, or one which will necessitate at the county's expense significant improvements to the minor road network. The county itself will have had a superordinate interest in seeing the road built, assuming a net benefit to the county as a whole and having a vested interest through its staffing of the Road Construction Unit.

HIGHWAY INQUIRY PROCEDURES

Two aspects of trunk road planning in the 1960s and 1970s have aggravated the polarity between local and regional or national considerations. One is the practice of holding inquiries or inviting participation on sections of a road separately. This has administrative convenience. But by assuming the existence of the road, it focuses attention on the purely local issues which are then seen to contain very restricted choices. Arguments appear merely parochial and objectors are given the impression of holding up for personal reasons a scheme of national importance which is already underway. It is possible that sheer embarrassment at being put into such an undignified position has added fuel to some campaigns against roads. The objectors' difficulty is twofold. At the Archway Inquiry in North London, for example, they had to accept that the short stretch of road proposed was a part of the London–Edinburgh–Thurso trunk road. Local objections seemed petty. At the same time such a road, with its complex, long-term and geographically dispersed effects, must have crucial second-order implications. The public is unlikely to be aware of them, even if it is allowed to discuss them.

The second aspect is the absence of a 'no-road' option. At one level the debate about proposals is isolated and localised. But at the higher national level it is assumed not to be necessary. It has been pointed out (Tyme 1975), for example, that between 1968 and 1975 Parliament had scarcely any opportunities to give adequate consideration to the national road strategy, despite the fact that such a strategy was supposedly the basis on which road plans were being proposed and justified. In the nineteenth century new railways and canals needed the authorisation of a Private Act of Parliament. Now the need for a road was not discussed democratically at any level. A string of conflicting attitudes emerged from the DOE when objectors tried to insist on discussing this at the inquiry stage. Improved access, or even sheer mobility for its own sake, on the part of those with private transport had come to be an assumed societal good. The pro-road lobby was enormously powerful (Hamer 1974). It also seems that the professions involved in road planning had developed the kind of self-justifying mystique which we see elsewhere as being inimical to participation.

This became particularly apparent at public inquiries, where people have often had the greatest difficulty in obtaining information without which they could not reasonably expect to evaluate and comment on proposals. Despite a ruling from the Council on Tribunals, questions were not allowed on the relation between a particular scheme and the relevant general policy. Road planning had become a centralised and technically complex matter. Objectors found that they had to know that certain technical information existed before they could hope to have access to it, and even then were subjected to delaying tactics. Information which was available on costs, engineering details, traffic counts and traffic projections was found to be open to correction. At the M3 Winchester Inquiry the Road Construction Unit was made to concede point after point (Wardroper 1978). The objectors at the M42 (Bromsgrove–Warwick) Inquiry went as far as the House of Lords in their fight against the subsequent ministerial decision. In the Appeal Court Lord Denning had referred to the need for natural justice at inquiries and for public confidence in them. Traffic forecasts were matters of fact, not policy as Whitehall claimed; and information coming to light after the inquiry (in this case a downward revision of design form standards) should be treated as pertinent to any appeal.

We referred in the previous chapter to the central position which inquiries hold in the history of participation, and the various dissatisfactions with them. Considerable changes have recently been promised in the case of highway inquiries (DTp 1978a). But they seem to have been provoked less by their inherent flaws than by the intervention and disruption of a single individual (Evans 1978; Sharman 1977; Tyme 1978). John Tyme's objectives were not altogether clear. But by taking the inquiry system as the Achilles heel of planning, he can now see a number of improvements.

In 1977 the Leitch Committee (DTp 1978b), concluded *inter alia* that the public should be given more and comprehensible information; that a road's environmental impact should be weighted more heavily; that existing traffic forecasting methods were suspect and their successors should be open to continued, careful scrutiny. The following year the Government conceded most of the points which had been at issue (DTp 1978a), and presented the first of an annual series of White Papers on national transport policies. Most recently the Leitch Committee has had to conclude that the Department of Transport's computer model for forecasting traffic on trunk roads should be abandoned because it does not work. Many of the complaints at inquiries in the 1970s had been directed precisely at the complexity and unchallengeable nature of such instruments.

It was through and by reason of the public inquiry system that these changes came about. The system itself remains virtually unchanged in its fundamentals. The action promised on highway inquiries meets many previous criticisms, but it amounts to little more than tidying up some obvious ragged edges. Given reasonable assumptions about the scope of participation in the late 1970s, the improved opportunities for objectors and others at highway inquiries are no more than might be expected.

The shortcomings in the administration of the road programme and the declining economic provision for its funding in the second half of the decade made it both inevitable and opportune to make changes to the participatory framework. But what of the inquiry system more generally? Many of the difficulties referred to in Chapter 4 persist. In addition, the organised and violent disruption of motorway inquiries suggests to some that the system should be changed radically. For example, an instrument such as the 'examination in public' of structure plans could become more general, with the issues and participants preselected by government. Other alternatives, such as the 'steering group' used in Bath from 1973 to avoid a public inquiry into the city's road proposals (Couger and Davis 1977), are also likely to be weak politically and unable to control the activities of authorities as the inquiry sometimes can. Many aspects of participation can be justified on the grounds that they smooth the potentially troubled waters of an inquiry. But the inquiry remains an important public right as a final resort.

PUBLIC TRANSPORT

Until recently the main opportunity for involvement in public transport provision, apart from structure plan participation, was through objection to the Traffic Commissioners, or through a Transport Users' Consultative Committee. The latter is an area-based watchdog for rail services. But in neither case has there been much activity. Only with the 1978 Transport Act and the introduction of a statutory duty on shire counties to produce a five-year, rolling Public Transport Plan (PTP), has there been an explicit opening for public comment, however limited.

The White Paper on transport policy (DTp 1977: 67) which preceded the Act pointed out that, 'more responsibility for planning transport to meet local needs should be devolved to local government since the most practical and democratic approach to co-ordination is local'. The need for devolution had been recognised ten years previously in another White Paper. But because nobody was given complete authority for public transport, and because financial incentives were partial and unco-ordinated, the policy had not been carried through.

The 1978 Act defines 'public transport' more broadly than before. Not only conventional road, rail and ferry services are included, but also school transport, hospital and welfare services, community buses, social car schemes, contract hire coaches, taxis and hire cars. A comprehensive and publicly available plan is looked for. A part of any PTP has to be the details of consultation with public transport operators, district councils and other county councils, and the consideration which has been given to their views (DTp 1978c). Only at the draft plan stage is there a wider opportunity for comment, for parish councils, trade unions, transport users' organisations and 'others appearing to the council to be specially concerned'. Only when the final plan is available are 'interested organisations and the general public' brought into the picture.

PTPs are intended to relate both to structure plans and to TPPs. In that respect the substance of any participation may have been pre-empted by these former plans. More important, however, is the fact that neither TPPs nor PTPs, unlike structure plans, give an opportunity for the public to comment until a plan has actually been produced; and even then there is no statutory requirement. Furthermore, the very existence of the PTP procedure involves an organised separation of transport modes. The subject of the most recent White Paper – *Policy for Roads: England* (DTp 1980) demonstrates a persistent refusal by central government to consider transport in an integrated fashion.

One of the key elements of the PTP is that it should give an account of the criteria applied to determine need. These criteria might well involve some form of participation. But actual practice is otherwise. Some counties have denied the possibility of establishing criteria – one even referring to need as 'an academic subject that cannot in practice be of any value' (Winfield 1979); others have specified a 'minimum level of service'; while others have used surveys to help them estimate the demand for public transport. Surveys have the advantage of filling the gap where otherwise people cannot express their needs: there is no parallel in transport for housing or hospital waiting lists. But there is a danger that surveys may intensify the tendency to treat transport as a market commodity rather than a service. Indeed the 'Market Analysis Project' has become one of the main tools of public transport planning. It includes a survey of passenger demand and of attitudes to travel by bus, as well as aggressive marketing techniques. When public involvement is discussed, it is at the level of publicity, of greater awareness of available services.

It could be argued that participation in transport planning is more vital than with other services. It has not yet been suggested that people are made homeless or deprived of educational or health facilities, as a direct result of policy. But their mobility has over the past two decades been severely diminished. Car ownership has risen steeply; but there are still some 45 per cent of the population without the use of a car. And because an increase in the use of the car has led to poorer public services, that 45 per cent often has no effective means of travelling except on foot or bicycle. Furthermore, there will always be a large minority who, because of age, income or disability, will never drive a car.

From the point of view of participation, there is an interesting lack of symmetry between transport and, for example, education or health services. The latter are enjoyed disproportionately more by the young or the old. But any cutback in the level and standard of provision is likely to be keenly opposed by the middle-aged, the parents or children of those who are being catered for. In the case of transport, however, it is particularly the middle-aged who enjoy the benefits; and they apparently see no reason to fight for increased mobility on behalf of their dependants. However, those who do have the greatest mobility – the middle-aged, middle-class males – are precisely that sector of the population which one is most likely to find in a participatory role elsewhere (Boaden *et al.* 1980).

And indeed they do participate in determining transport policy, through their economic power to own and use a car. Car ownership is assumed to be an expression of the public will, an unarguable good. But whether car ownership operates at an individual or corporate level (viz. the large number of company cars), it does so against the interests of relatively powerless groups which make up nearly half the population. It is as though private education and health care had expanded to such an extent that there were scarcely any teachers or doctors left to man the public sector.

Any attempt at genuine participation must involve a self-conscious awareness of the issues at hand. This seems to be generally missing in the case of transportation. Individual car ownership or use prevents people from appreciating that it is more dangerous, more energy-consuming, more toxic and more expensive than the collective alternative – public transport. There is no mechanism for alerting the individual to the fact that he enjoys his mobility by reason of financial support from government to the car industry, tax exemption on firms' cars, low duty on petrol, inflated subsidies for road transport, and so on. Awareness of the consequences of alternative policy options is important in any participatory exercise. The transport example shows just how self-interest may obscure that awareness.

RURAL TRANSPORT AND SELF-HELP

One of the most important characteristics of transportation is its urban–rural split. In the cities motorways and other new roads often proved objectionable, despite the clear benefit of greater mobility to the car-owning population, because of the land and particularly the houses which they took. In rural areas the disruption was to amenity and to agricultural interests. But the split is more pronounced over public transport. The mobility of inner city residents, especially the poor and elderly, can be severely restricted for cross-town journeys. The establishment of PTAs and PTEs was intended to re-shape urban travel. It was only ten years later that rural problems were taken into account.

The rural population increased by nearly one-fifth between 1961 and 1977. A disproportionate number of them are old or unemployed compared with urban residents. Life is more expensive outside towns. Nearly all services (school, post-office, medical facilities, etc.) are at a distance, having moved to more central locations at the same time as the demand on public transport became too small to support it. The inverse relation between car ownership and viable public transport is even more marked in rural areas. Car ownership is higher, but its use to take the head of household to work leaves wives and children immobile for much of the time.

The wider definition of public transport in the 1978 Act was designed in part to tackle the rural problem. At the same time, fifteen experimental schemes (RUTEX) were set up by central government during 1977–78 in Scotland, Wales, North Yorkshire and Devon (DTp 1978d). They ranged from a flexible version of a conventional bus service, run by a national operator, to the use of private cars run by a local voluntary committee and private motorists. Other schemes used minibuses as postbuses or school buses, with fixed routes and schedules; and pre-booked, shared hire-cars to take passengers to nearby buses and trains or to hospitals and doctors.

In other areas, East Anglia for example, services have been set up which involve co-operation between several bodies. A bus company will provide vehicles, maintenance and driver-training, the county council a grant, and the local community produces the drivers and a committee to manage day-to-day running. Typically a twelve-seater minibus will connect half-a-dozen villages to the various facilities in neighbouring towns, which they lack. Such schemes have been helped by their drivers' exemption in the 1978 Transport Act from needing a Public Service Vehicle (PSV) driving licence. It is possible now for private operators to advertise and charge fares.

Participation at the point of delivery of a service can be a two-edged weapon, as the National Consumer Council has pointed out (NCC 1978). Against the possible benefits of voluntary group activity, user identification and community involvement, lies the danger that performance will be sacrificed to cost effectiveness. Authorities may be tempted to replace conventional with unconventional services for the savings which can be made on subsidies. But there is evidence that the stability and quality of service may suffer. Furthermore, unconventional forms of public transport contribute most where existing transport provision is already high, and in fairly robust communities – a pool of sixteen trained drivers is needed, for example, to ensure continuity of service for a village bus. Some village communities will also find that in the summer months they are providing a service for tourists rather than themselves.

The experience with RUTEX shows that people have adapted quite quickly to the withdrawal of conventional services. The number who will then use the alternatives is too small to justify in general much more than a car-based scheme. Car-sharing or car-pooling for the journey to work, which has now been made legal, is likely to become more beneficial in urban or suburban areas. 'Dial-a-ride' and community minibuses are expensive to run; school buses are only available, economically, on term-time weekdays at peak hours; postbuses are only effective for long, straight routes, such as in Scotland.

These rural experiments can be seen as part of a more general campaign to promote alternatives such as 'paratransit'. Jitneys, park-and-ride, minitram, etc. are proposed as solutions to urban transport problems. We shall see in the next chapter that alternative forms of tenure have been proposed as a solution to housing problems. But in neither case is it clear that alternatives as such are what is required. There may be advantages from a participatory viewpoint – though technology and control mechanisms will not be developed for that alone. RUTEX found that where a scheme did work the greatest contribution came from the enthusiasm of volunteers. Whether this kind of direct involvement or self-help should be considered as participation is debatable. We shall meet the question again when we discuss housing and the health service. But at least it does imply the active understanding and response to a problem of service delivery which one expects to find as one component of participation.

Housing differs from other local government services with which we deal in this book in a number of respects. There is an enormous variation in the scale and organisation of different housing authorities and in the nature of their problems. 'Housing' can subsume a wide range of activities, but may not do so in all authorities – for example, design, maintenance, rent collection, loans, improvement, and slum clearance. These activities may impinge critically on the function of other local government departments though the implications of any potential relationship often remain obscure.

Housing differs from, say, education or social services, in being more obviously focused on physical provision while simultaneously fulfilling fundamental human and social needs. Furthermore it does not offer a universal service. Owner-occupiers, the 'undeserving', and others who do not present themselves are explicitly excluded from consideration. Traditionally, public housing, which today accounts for about one-third of the total, has been seen as a social response to need, an alternative to the private market response to demand. But because of its philanthropic and somewhat patronising origins, 'need' is defined in its manifest form and according to rather particular notions of who the deserving poor may be.

Housing authorities have tended to be merely reactive and in the past have neglected to search out and cater for hidden housing needs, such as those of one-person households. Where any scope remained after slum clearance and rehousing, attention was focused on large or low-income families and the homeless. The plight of those who were driven from the shrinking private rental market in recent years was not given adequate attention. A weakness of housing as a local government service is that the authority's structure does not encourage it to know and understand the full housing position in its area and to take responsibility for it. Even if the planning department has the necessary information and intentions, they may not be shared by the housing, architects' and other departments which need to be involved. The sense of responsibility is further weakened by the way in which central government persists in treating housing as a national rather than a local problem.

An opportunity for the public to discuss local government housing policy does not readily present itself. Structure plan participation covers such a wide field of topics that a specific area, housing for example, can be lost. The topics of transportation, housing and recreation emerged as superordinate matters of concern in one structure plan case-study (Stringer 1978) both in a random sample survey of the electorate and among those who actually sent in comments on the plan in question. But each topic occupied less than 10 per cent of the plan documentation and publicity. Structure planning is a poor vehicle for bringing to the front a discussion of housing policy, in terms which the public will readily understand. Structure plans are unusually complex documents and topics are treated as highly interdependent on one another. Moreover, the structure planning authority, the county, is not the housing authority. From a policy viewpoint, of course, housing cannot be tackled as a separate question. The dilemma is how to present issues for participation with sufficient simplicity to promote understanding, but without obscurity and thereby pre-empting the consideration of interrelated issues.

In practice we shall see that more realistic opportunities for participation in housing lie at the local level. In the private sector people have become involved in commenting on proposals which affect the more general housing environment, particularly in the context of the areal approach to housing underlying statutorily governed General Improvement Areas and Housing Action Areas. Participation here belies over-simple distinctions between planning and housing as local government activities. Council tenants may also be involved in this way. But where authorities have given opportunities for tenant participation in management, they have tended to be concerned with rather narrower considerations of the housing itself and its maintenance. Tenant participation has been encouraged in various ways by central government during the 1970s. Statutory provisions are included in the 1980 Housing Act.

But before we discuss these opportunities and provisions in any detail, we shall paint in the background to housing as a public service, and in particular the role of local government and its housing management function.

HOUSING AS A PUBLIC SERVICE

At the beginning of the First World War only one-half of 1 per cent of the housing stock was municipally owned and virtually all of it had been built since the 1890 Housing of the Working Classes Act. Public housing began in earnest in 1919. 'Homes fit for Heroes' was the slogan. Between the wars an annual average of nearly 70,000 houses was built, and many more than that in the private sector. The main points of development and change were the shift in the 1930 'Greenwood' Act from general needs construction to clearance and redevelopment, and a concentration in the 1935 Act on problems of overcrowding.

Inevitably these goals were interrupted in 1939. Post-war, an estimated 1.25 million new houses were required, in addition to a considerable repair and maintenance programme. It was not until the mid-1950s that local authorities were encouraged to turn their attention once again to slum clearance and to overspill building. General needs were henceforward to be left to the private sector, where renewal was to be stimulated by grants for improvement. Clearance quickly gathered momentum and was further encouraged by the 1961 Housing Act. Between 1954 and 1973 it persisted at a relatively high level.

The subsequent downturn in this policy and a mounting criticism of clearance programmes coincided with the general rise of participatory movements in the early 1970s. The destruction of communities and the socially insensitive haste (or delays) of clearance programmes were certainly frequent targets. But more influential was a recognition that the policy was not able to keep abreast of the problem. Economic recession in the years since 1975 made improvement and rehabilitation seem an even more attractive alternative to clearance and reconstruction.

Grants for improvement had been introduced as early as 1949, for houses of an expected life of 30 years or more. But it was not until the 1954 Housing Repairs and Rents Act that serious attention was paid to dilapidation. However, take-up was largely by owner-occupiers; while the physical and social problems which the Act was intended to tackle lay largely in the private rental sector. The 1964 Act introduced powers to compel landlords to improve their property, but its procedures proved too cumbersome to apply generally. This Act's greater significance ultimately lay in the duty it imposed on local authorities to inspect their domain and identify areas for comprehensive improvement. It was this initiative which was extended by the 1969 Act to lay emphasis on voluntary improvement, higher levels of grant, grants for environmental improvement and the powers to declare General Improvement Areas. From many points of view the shift from clearance to improvement is central to an understanding of housing policy, not least in respect of participation.

THE ROLE OF LOCAL GOVERNMENT

Since 1919 housing has traditionally been a local service, despite political attempts to define it as a national problem and to develop overall programmes. The ministerial role in housing has been weak, even though central government approval is often required by local authorities. Control is exercised in practice mainly by means of subsidies and loan sanction. The wish of post-war governments to exercise more control is perhaps indicated by the average of one major Housing Act every two years. The post-war faith in planning led to the public sector rather than speculative building being seen as the main instrument through which any policy could be implemented.

Until 1949 local authorities' task was to provide housing for the working classes. In that year they were empowered to provide for any people in housing need; as well as to give financial aid to private owners for improvement. In the 1960s, however, the tasks of housing the needy and helping to maintain a viable, general housing stock diverged again. Concern at the decline of the private rental sector had led through a series of measures to the development of a stronger housing society movement (housing associations, co-operatives). Initially this offered below-market rents, but soon turned to building and managing houses for people who could meet their cost. Housing associations have shown great variety, from large quasi-commercial concerns to small one-project initiatives; and with objectives ranging from paternalistic homes for the elderly to Shelter-backed schemes. For administrative reasons, housing associations are not popular with local authorities and have largely been left to go their own way.

Since the Second World War owner-occupation has greatly increased. Now local authorities often find that their role has reverted to providing housing for the poor; and in particular handling the allocation of tenants to the dilapidated or unpopular stock which has accumulated. The failure to develop comprehensive housing policies has meant that other bodies (e.g. the Housing Corporation) have increasingly taken over other functions which local authorities might have exercised. It is in this light that housing management has to be viewed.

HOUSING MANAGEMENT

The responsibilities of housing authorities after 1919 were carried out as a service with unusually imprecise boundaries. Early on, housing provision was often simply added to existing functions such as public health or civil engineering. By the Second World War only some 20 per cent of local authorities had appointed housing managers. Housing might be managed through a council's clerk, treasurer, medical officer, engineer or surveyor, either singly or in harness. The diversity of possible functions of a housing department made it all the more difficult to establish a separate identity for it. For example, even in existing housing departments, applications, lettings, rent collection, ordering repairs, executing repairs, estate supervision, and housing welfare can variously be, but are never invariably, their responsibility.

As a result, housing management has suffered a lack of respect within local government, as well as in its own eyes and those of the public. It has had low status, confused or conflicting objectives and unpopular tasks to perform. Housing managers are seldom chief officers and rarely on a local authority's management team. In that now highly professionalised atmosphere, housing management has not been regarded by others as a profession. The present Institute of Housing is only ten years old and very few housing staff belong to it. Membership rests on gaining the IOH Diploma, which older staff do not have. It has proved difficult to attract graduates or trainees, for whom the pay and training opportunities are poor.

Despite a series of urgent calls at a national level over the past ten or more years for a scheme of education and training for all levels of the housing service, very little has been done. The Institute has no clear, comprehensive policy. The idea of a Central Housing Training Council has been abandoned. In 1979 central government announced that authorities must make their own arrangements. Outside London, which has its own association of borough housing officers, there is little activity. Training is usually justified in terms of increased efficiency but it could also help staff resolve their confused identity. If an emphasis were placed on human relations and social skills training, a more participatory approach to management might follow.

The two professional bodies which existed before 1939 reflected one aspect of the identity problem. The Society of Women Housing Managers stressed the social side of housing, while the Institute of Housing concentrated on property management. Today the IOH Diploma is ignored by many younger staff because it emphasises law and building technology at the cost of the social side. Housing is a multidisciplinary field, but has largely failed to develop a comprehensive service. The 'accountant' who wants to reduce rent arrears struggles with the 'building manager' who is concerned about vandalism; and the 'social psychologist' who would help people to choose and manage their own housing is left in a corner. Championing the cause of the disadvantaged or using council housing to compensate for social deficits is not as clear a goal as in social services departments.

Local authorities' original housing management function, post-1919, was to avoid unsatisfactory tenants and provide for 'respectable' families. Local autonomy, an excess of demand for the product and the absence of clearly defined administrative procedures made the development of paternalistic, conservative and restrictive practices only too likely. With changes in the function of public housing in recent decades, more of the managerial task has come to focus on administering 'problem families' and unsatisfactory dwellings. The problem then is how to help the deprived – the chronically unemployed, single-parent families, racial minorities – without simply allocating them the worst housing. With these difficulties, there is unlikely to be much spare attention for innovations of a participatory kind.

PARTICIPATION IN URBAN RENEWAL AND HOUSING

One of the main issues in post-war housing policy has increasingly been that of decay and modernisation. We have also suggested that participation in housing, as in planning, can more realistically be conceived as occurring at a local level. These themes are brought together in the areal approach to improvement through General Improvement Areas (GIAs) and Housing Action Areas (HAAs) (DOE 1975a). But before discussing this approach as an instrument of central government policy, we shall look at a well-documented example (Paris and Blackaby 1979) of how one city council responded in the early 1970s and how it sought to involve residents in urban renewal policy to an extent that had previously been rare. If participation now seemed desirable, it was because of a wish to avoid past mistakes and, more particularly, to legitimise a policy of housing improvement as against development. Paris and Blackaby's study highlights the achievements of Birmingham's programme, as well as a number of failings of general interest.

Participation was proposed as an objective in its own right as well as a means of policy development. Two levels of policy were instituted, local and city level. Councillors, officers and project-team members engaged in intensive contacts with inner city residents. Some were enthusiastic members of local residents' organisations and became committed to the preparation of plans for their neighbourhood. At the city level: 'With a regular attendance of between ten and twenty residents' representatives at liaison meetings with the urban renewal subcommittee, and the wide network of contacts this represented, it was impossible for the city council to ignore the strength of feeling and arguments put forward' (Paris and Blackaby 1979: 146).

The two levels of participation drew attention to the difficulty which can face locally based groups and organisations when the issues at stake are not limited to or determined by the locality. At the city level should they claim priority status, attempt to change the general policy or voluntarily forgo their claim? GIAs and HAAs such as those in which Birmingham participants lived are usually designated and managed in a more piecemeal fashion. Residents are invited to consider only whether they wish their own neighbourhood to be improved; or perhaps, because they are private tenants, to opt for redevelopment and public rehousing. Debate and trade-off have to be conducted within the immediate community only, where, however fraught with personal overtones, it is at least more meaningful for the politically unsophisticated.

These difficulties reflect more fundamental problems which underlie areally based approaches. Independently of participatory efforts, issues of prioritisation, redistribution and class divisiveness are inescapable. Different considerations operate, of course, as between the designation and implementation of GIAs and HAAs. They are more complex contexts than may at first sight appear for any far-reaching attempt at participation.

Managerially, the comprehensive approach in Birmingham faced several problems which affected participation. They would be less likely in a more piecemeal programme. A large number of local authority departments can be involved in a GIA or HAA. Where several projects are developed simultaneously, co-ordinating their contributions and agreement can be complex. In one case a single department successfully countermanded a scheme which had been passed by other departments and by the residents. Through the form of the housing-area processes which it statutorily imposed on local authorities, central government placed significant controls on the way they relate their activities to neighbourhoods in need, but it has not ensured that corporate administrative machinery is available.

Central government indirectly affected participation in another way. The urban renewal programme in Birmingham was a very limited and slow success because adequate resources simply were not available. Disillusion among the public was inevitable. Schemes are less likely to prove overambitious if they are limited to one or two areas at a time.

In this large-scale scheme a hierarchy of responsibility emerged among the council's officers. It tended to be the junior officers who worked in the neighbourhood project teams; and juniors who had the most intensive contact with residents in housing visits, inspections and housing allocations. They assisted the residents in the formation of associations and the preparation of plans. On smaller schemes or in smaller authorities quite senior officers might take on these tasks. Paris and Blackaby point out that the juniors' previous responsibility to senior officers was replaced by a dual relationship with seniors and with the public. This introduced tensions when officers felt unable to maintain neutrality and moved towards being either an official mouthpiece or a residents' mediator; and even to resignation from the job. Undoubtedly it is valuable for the electorate to be disabused of the 'them' and 'us' notion, and to see disagreements between officers or between officers and councillors. But the lesson can be disruptive of more immediate goals.

GENERAL IMPROVEMENT AND HOUSING ACTION AREAS

'One of the most challenging aspects of the 1969 Housing Act was the need to organise public participation in General Improvement Areas.' These are the opening words of a DOE Improvement Note on public participation (DOE 1973b). Challenging, indeed, since the Act goes no further than to specify a duty to publish information. The greater part of the Note and most other reports of GIA experience concentrate on techniques of data collection, publicity and promotion – such as social surveys, public meetings and exhibitions. It is difficult not to interpret many participatory efforts as successful sales campaigns with very thorough and responsive market research backing. Where they have gone further it has been because the local government officers have not been bound simply by the more obvious interpretation of the statute book, nor by the narrow, professional concerns for efficiency.

Central government has offered encouragement. The authors of the Note referred to above felt able to say, even if without supporting evidence: 'Perhaps the most important success of public participation however has been in providing a further link between council and residents and thus helping to overcome the apathy and 'we–they' cynicism which can affect people's attitudes to local government' (DOE 1973b). In later circulars the attitude is reinforced that a successful GIA is more than a high take-up of improvement grants and improvements approved by the residents in the form of tree planting and small-scale traffic management. For example: 'Almost invariably, a residents' committee can play more than a merely consultative role; they can indeed provide a very useful addition to the authority's resources for carrying through a project. Participation should ideally lead to the identification and use of resources which will continue to make a contribution to the welfare of the neighbourhood long after the initial process of area improvement has been completed' (DOE 1975a: Memo C, para. 33).

The Department of the Environment has found (DOE 1978a) that successful GIAs have typically been of the order of 2–300 houses. Housing and environmental improvement at this level can be a means to promote an active interest in the community and a more aware relationship between local government and the electorate. From a number of standpoints GIAs seem to be an ideal participatory vehicle, and many have been very successful in that respect. But a disadvantage is that they focus on limited areas, without reference to competition within the town as a whole. The issues at hand are depoliticised. So long as individual streets and neighbourhoods gain some satisfaction for their local grievances, they may miss sight of more general urban problems. Furthermore, it must be admitted that participation is incidental to their primary purpose, and they would not be retained as an instrument of policy in order to promote it. Although 977 were in operation by May 1977, of a potential of several thousands, they have since been cut back.

Participation is even more crucial in Housing Action Areas, which were introduced in 1974. They required special action in the interests of the residents, with attention being paid to social conditions as much as to the physical structure of housing. It was understood that if the well-being of the residents was at issue they should be involved in the nature and timing of the proposed action. To suggest that social criteria were as or more important than the physical criteria in housing was revolutionary.

But initial progress with HAAs was slow, particularly in the private rented sector. By 1978 the 350 or so HAAs which had been declared included less than 20 per cent of the dwellings which had originally been considered suitable for intensive treatment. More recently, rising costs and the diversion of government policy to the sale of public housing have impeded momentum. Cost limits, compulsory improvement powers, the acquisition of property for improvement and the indifference of building societies were stumbling blocks in the HAA procedure. In many cases the very notion of rehabilitation no longer inspired confidence. The opposition to clearance was never demonstrably universal. The extent of these difficulties was particularly damaging for participation. In areas of chronic stress, if confidence is to be built, activity needs to be maximised immediately after an HAA has been designated. Cooperation needs to be promoted and improvement visibly concentrated. An open approach is needed, with area offices and individually identifiable officers. None of this is easy for an authority to implement in the face of the difficulties mentioned.

HOUSING STRATEGIES AND INVESTMENT PROGRAMMES

The introduction in 1977 of Housing Strategies and Investment Programmes (HIPs) emphasised a more concentrated approach to urban problems. It was intended in part to prevent action areas from being geographically and strategically isolated (DOE 1977) Local authorities were to present, annually, co-ordinated analyses of their housing conditions and to formulate coherent policies and programmes of capital spending. This was to be an opportunity for a comprehensive and flexible approach to housing in both public and private sectors. The scheme is (crudely) comparable to the TPPs discussed in the previous chapter; and, in its strategic aspect, to structure planning.

Within HIP national housing objectives are to be met, under conditions of local autonomy and financial control. Their formulation is presented as part of the local policy process. But DOE circulars of guidance to local authorities on the HIPs' procedure have been ambivalent about public involvement. The initial assumption was that authorities would wish to consider how to develop existing consultation 'with those who are able to contribute to the formulation and interpretation of their housing strategy'. Just how restrictive that body of consultees could be was subsequently revealed: few authorities sought more than a cursory involvement, if that, even on the part of elected members, and they had their knuckles rapped for the neglect (Bramley *et al.* 1979; DOE 1978b). Fewer made efforts to discuss their housing strategy or the overall impact of policies with representative groups of the public. Most were in favour of publicising HIPs' submissions, as the DOE circulars of 1978 and 1979 encouraged them to do. But in the absence of specific guidance on how to approach the public, authorities appeared at a loss.

Here, even more clearly than in the case of TPPs or structure plans, public participation becomes a victim of rationalisation and efficiency and of central–local government relations at officer level. The procedure was seen as anything from merely another statistical return to Whitehall, to a bid for resources. The objective of gaining financial control over their housing policy became paramount for local authorities. The complexity of the process and forms encouraged them in the belief that not only the general public, but also the elected member, would find them too difficult to understand. But such defeatism, and the possible consequential loss of local democratic control over housing policy, is not necessary. A few authorities have run seminars or produced explanatory documents, for members at least, and have given them the chance to see housing policy as an interrelated system.

TENANT PARTICIPATION

Although GIAs (but not HAAs) may contain houses owned by a local authority, the most significant opportunity for participation in the public housing sector has been in schemes for tenant participation. It has been legally possible since 1936 for tenants to be involved with management. But this has become more widespread in the 1970s. The 1980 Housing Act makes tenant participation a statutory obligation of local authorities, though they will be left to decide the details of its implementation.

Earlier, in 1948, the National Association of Tenants and Residents was founded; and in 1957 a London tenants' organisation (to become the Association of London Housing Estates in 1965) was formed. The latter body now has some 200 affiliated groups. By 1975 a survey (Richardson and Kendall 1975) found that 41 per cent of housing authorities had some kind of tenant participation scheme; though only 13 per cent had a formal scheme such as tenant involvement in council committees. The schemes were to be found disproportionately more often in London boroughs. One account (Hayes 1963) of tenants' associations in London in the late 1950s and early 1960s concluded that they could play a valuable part in community organisation. Their success appeared to depend on a non-paternalistic, permissive and encouraging attitude on the part of the local authority. The housing manager needed to be alive to the potential for the formation of an association, often on the basis of a single, commonly felt grievance; to see it through the early period with tact and patience; but to make it clear that ultimately the tenants must be responsible for their own association. Persistence and stability were more possible than is sometimes believed. Of 58 groups in London in 1962, for example, 39 had been in existence for longer than ten years, and a further 18 for more than five years.

The motives for these schemes can be variously attributed. The earlier tenants' association movement, campaigning as a pressure group for tenants' rights, was likely to lead to an incorporative form of participation in the 1970s, given the general trends elsewhere in government. Certainly the issues for tenants had not lessened by then – insufficient maintenance, deteriorating properties, unnecessarily poor architecture, and a patronising and mystifying style of housing management which denied them even the right to redecorate their homes. Management itself felt the two former burdens, as well as diseconomies of scale and an inflexibility of response to changing demands in a very large service. But the style of management, whatever problems it laboured under, caused particular frustrations for tenants. Managers' practice when faced with their clients is to emphasise their own knowledge, competence and control. Housing needs are individualised, effectively withdrawing group support of various kinds. The discussion of policy is reduced to specifics and local protests. The 'queue' and the 'points' system create an atmosphere of grand ordeal supervised by a dark and omnipotent tyrant. The complexities of the administrative system or its self-evident character to the managers, defeat attempts to gain an explanation, and invariably leave a taste of secrecy and injustice.

Technical and institutionalised forms of participation cannot overcome these problems. As in other fields dealt with in this book, professional re-education is called for. For the moment one usually finds that schemes of tenant participation offer a forum for the discussion of problems, and a hope from management that this will remove some of the burden of maintenance and improve relations with tenants. Formal schemes have been of four types: co-option on to, or advisory membership of, the housing committee (one-third of the members may be tenants); a similar status on a housing sub-committee, with no limits as to numbers and with delegated executive powers; membership, usually shared with councillors, of a special advisory or consultative committee; or attendance at regular discussion meetings on housing management, without formal committee status.

A rather more extensive scheme was the one proposed for Thamesmead in South East London (Simpson 1976). A Co-Management Body (CMB) was to

be set up with both advisory and executive roles, and ... a contractual relationship between the CMB and the [Greater London Council] ... established, together with a formal role for the CMB in the consultation process. A major publicity campaign to ensure that the concept of the CMB was fully understood by residents was also recommended. It was intended that at first the CMB should undertake an advisory role in management, including basic tenancy conditions and the letting of estate shops, as well as in areas such as education, employment, communications and transport. In view of the experimental nature of the scheme it was agreed that there should be only a limited transfer of executive duties in the first instance: these would include certain maintenance services (internal redecorations, repairs and some environmental maintenance), a Thamesmead Mutual Exchange Bureau, management of estate facilities such as clubrooms, drying rooms and playgroups, and responsibilities in general areas such as the control of dogs, garden competitions, regulation of parking and a residents' Suggestion Scheme.

Such arrangements have the virtue of institutionalising regular interaction between decision-makers and those who live with the results of their decisions. The council cannot avoid an awareness of tenant opinion. A limited number of tenants, who serve as representatives, have the opportunity for new and valuable political experience. Some improvements in standards of maintenance and the provision of new amenities have inevitably occurred. The more exact extent of achievement is difficult to gauge from the sparse information available.

On the face of it, there are likely to be a number of problems. The two parties may have conflicting aims and unrealistic expectations. Tenant control is a long-te_m goal and one which the authority may not share. Tenants will look for improvements to their own estate and be bored by the grievances or competing demands of others. The councils may expect more constructive help than untrained people could be expected to offer. Although the concern is a political one, both parties insist on defining their interests as social and apolitical. Tenant representatives, however, are faced with a difficult task. They have to manage feedback to a relatively uninterested constituency and still maintain their own representative credibility with the council. Faced with an apathetic constituency, a sceptical council, and a complex and unfamiliar administrative system, the temptation to become incorporated into the machinery and to adopt the housing manager's perspective must be strong.

On the face of it, housing tenancy seems a particularly good potential context for participation. G.D.H. Cole saw the workplace as the prime focus. After a job, everyone wants a decent home. Despite management pressures to individualise the tenant's status, there is a basis for a collective and common interest. The motivation, opportunities and skills for participation might seem as high here as anywhere.

But one recent empirical evaluation (Andrews 1979) is pessimistic about the chances that formal schemes could improve tenant–landlord relations in the short term. Four reasons are given. The sponsoring organisation, the local authority, is likely to be dominant in the scheme, making the rules and controlling the procedures. In many instances, including the case under evaluation, there is insufficient community organisation even of an informal kind to act as a channel for participation. Many of the residents' most important demands will be unacceptable to officers and councillors: for example, residents' involvement in the ordering of priorities for maintenance and lettings. Finally, for anything more than token participation, both parties must radically realign their roles and relationships. It is concluded that the tenant finds it as difficult to re-order his subordinate and labelled position as does the officer to accept the tenant as a colleague. The solution recommended is reform within the authority's housing management.

It is unfortunate that this is an asymmetrical solution. However far-reaching the reform, the tenants are likely to be invited to participate in their own local activities. Although professional and administrative reform is essential, if that is the only concern the emphasis will be on finding appropriate forms and procedures for a replicable system. Given the variety of housing demands and expectations and the differing resources which tenants have available, a more open and flexible approach will be necessary which is not afraid to assert the validity of unique solutions. This approach would seek to locate or generate, and subsequently stimulate, whatever local energies were available to whatever ends were feasible. The ultimate aim, though, may well be seen as the tenants' own development as citizens, as working people in control of all aspects of their lives; rather than simply more efficient, or even more humane, housing management.

At the time of writing tenant participation is the most alive and present issue of those we deal with in this book, due to the provisions contained in the 1980 Housing Act. Although promoted by a Conservative Government, the provisions closely reflect Labour's 1977 Green Paper on Housing Policy. There, tenant control was prompted as much by escalating costs of unit management and maintenance as by any respect for tenant status. The Act requires landlord authorities to keep tenants informed of 'substantive matters of housing management', enable them to comment on them and to consider their comments. They are to provide information about processes of housing allocation. These collective arrangements are in addition to the greater emphasis given to individual rights, such as security of tenure and the right to carry out improvements.

Several points which were raised about these clauses by the Standing Committee are interesting in highlighting particular intentions of the legislation and some differences between housing and other local services *vis-à-vis* participation. The level of rents, for example, is not a matter for consultation. Yet people would doubtless feel more strongly that this should be a matter for comment than, say, rail fares or the construction costs of a motorway, where there is consultation. The Act covers existing stock and the people in it. Although consultation about demolition and improvement is allowed for, construction is excluded. It is assumed that the provision of new housing is not an issue; indeed depleting the stock by the sale of council houses is one of the legislation's main targets. But it was still possible to refer in Committee to instances where tenants had been directly involved in housing design (e.g. in Wandsworth and Islington London boroughs), which would be difficult to parallel for other services. The official attitude, however, to which we shall return, is that tenant participation in design can be no more than feedback: existing tenants commenting on their dwellings, for the benefit of architects of future buildings – irrespective, presumably, of changing circumstances.

The crux, though, is what constitutes housing management. Traditionally, construction has not been included. Would high-rise or deck-access have been built otherwise? But more importantly the Act gives landlord authorities considerable discretion to decide what constitutes management. And that at the same time as severe setbacks introduced by government to plans for promoting the training and re-training of housing managers. The two policies are not necessarily contradictory. But given the complaints levied at the young profession, the rapidly changing function of council housing, and the number of non-housing issues which impinge upon it, a little more clarity might have been expected. Participation in housing management, then, must be ill-defined.

The proposed legislation has a strong enabling element, as in the case of planning. But the discretionary principle, which underlies many central–local government relations, has strengths and weaknesses. Much is made of the advantages of flexibility, the opportunity for authorities to gain and share experience, and the tailoring of participation to local circumstances. Central government adopts pupil-centred teaching! But sometimes it hands out potentially dangerous equipment with insufficient instructions.

It is suggested, for example, that a tenants' committee for the whole of an authority's stock should be set up, which would be consulted on major changes in management policy or practice. It should not be too large, but should be representative both of different estates and of dwelling types. The committee is a forum for discussion, with an advisory role. It would keep itself informed of the general tenant viewpoint, possibly 'by twice-yearly public meetings'.

The questions of representation and representativeness loom large here. We shall return to them when discussing health service provision. In a large authority a committee constituted on such a basis would inevitably be cumbersome and out of touch with tenants. Its lack of executive function is not likely to impress tenants that it has teeth. These difficulties could be softened by a hierarchy of more local committees, which at the estate level might be given some specific duties (as under certain existing schemes). But the issues remain of how central committee members' representative identity relates to that of district or county councillors; and of how they could exercise a representative role in practice. There is a danger that committees which have a limited basis and responsibilities are seen as a façade to conceal the lack of possibilities for public involvement.

CO-OPERATIVE HOUSING TENURE AND HOUSING ASSOCIATIONS

An element of flexibility in participative housing had been introduced by central government in the mid-1970s when it not only encouraged authorities and housing associations to turn their attention to tenant participation but also set the 'co-operative' ball rolling. A form of co-operative housing had existed since 1961. But the difficulty with co-ownership societies was that members had to meet the full cost of their dwellings. Without a direct subsidy they were beyond the means of low income families.

A housing co-operative of this kind has been described (Campbell 1976) as follows:

> ... an association where members are the tenants who together, not individually, own the flats and/or homes in which they live. Through their association they negotiate a group mortgage for which they are jointly or corporately responsible. Each pays to the co-operative a rent for his dwelling based on an appropriate proportion of the loan charges plus an amount for management and maintenance. They elect from themselves a committee to run their affairs and may retain whatever staff or engage whatever professional or other services considered necessary to enable them to perform their executive functions properly.

Apart from co-ownership there are two other types of co-operative. In a non-equity co-operative, the tenants own or lease the property collectively, but have no share in the equity. The tenant takes out a share on entering the co-op, which he redeems at its original value on leaving. A management co-operative gives tenants responsibility for some or all management functions but they have no ownership interest. The key to these forms of co-op is finance. The 1975 Housing Rents and Subsidies Act made it possible for local authorities to promote tenants' co-operatives in a variety of ways and transfer normal council housing subsidies to the co-op.

A former chairman of the Holloway Tenants' Co-operative in London (Housing Review 1975) has referred to

> ... the close personal involvement which lay at the heart of the co-op's success. The tenants' management group was on the spot and repairs could often be done on the same day. Conversion plans were discussed with the individuals who would live in the completed flats and often when there was some doubt about a scheme being approved, e.g. if it involved a roof conversion, they would lobby the neighbours to support the application. Allocations had not been a problem. Often members who were themselves awaiting rehousing would serve on the committee (which visited all

prospective tenants to check on their conditions) and vote against themselves in the face of greater needs.

The possibilities are clearly there, even if this is probably too rosy a picture – particularly, for example, on the question of allocations, which, when they involve minority groups, are more of a problem than in Holloway. Unfortunately, there is no evidence that co-operatives have gone beyond being a fashion stimulated by an enthusiastic Minister. Part of the problem lies in the complicated financial arrangements which underpin them – an instance of the generally tangled web which central government has spun for housing. In addition, co-operatives make even more demands for professional realignment on the part of housing managers and other local authority departments. As in the case of tenant participation, participants' aims have often proved to be short term. Once they are achieved, interest wanes. Responsibilities are allowed to fall back on to the shoulders of someone who is seen as willing to do the job or is paid to do it.

The extent to which co-operative tenure is or could be participatory is open to question on other grounds. The Working Party on Housing Co-operatives (DOE 1975b) was at pains to urge local authorities and housing associations to embark on tenant participation. They saw a tenancy which would assume appropriate responsibilities as a prerequisite for establishing a co-operative. But they also referred to the viewpoint that it was preferable to institute full co-operatives independently of initial, participatory schemes. Although it was recognised that participation must give practical outcomes rather than be a talking shop, no advice was offered as to how this was to be achieved. The basis of co-operatives, particularly under current plans to help all tenants buy their own homes, highlights the tendency for participation in the provision of a service like housing to slide over into consumerism.

Housing associations existed in the nineteenth century. Since 1919 local authorities have been able to gain subsidies to promote them. But, as with co-operatives, they came to the fore in the 1970s as a part of the general desire for alternative forms of tenure and for grass-roots initiatives. The desire for alternatives, whether actual or potential, informs nearly all drives for participation. But the solution to perceived problems is more important than alternative institutions as such. There is little likelihood that problems referred to in this chapter, such as insensitive management, the exclusion of certain groups from the housing market, or class fragmentation by tenure differences, will be solved by alternative forms of tenure. The problems are more likely to dissolve the alternatives. Housing associations may be incorporated by local authorities, who otherwise see them as competitors, too independent, administratively untidy, or redundant. Or they may effectively be eliminated by turning over their stock to private ownership. Similarly, the Housing Corporation, which initially gave confidence to the concept of co-operatives as an alternative, has recently become involved in issues such as inner city rehabilitation or special need housing. However important such problems are, by pursuing them the Housing Corporation tends to become a part of the central government machinery rather than a means to genuine alternatives, with potential for participation.

PARTICIPATORY DESIGN AND SELF-BUILD

Most forms of tenant participation are liable to involve more than just an authority's housing department, at least from the tenants' point of view. Experience of participation has shown that members of the public do not see their world as divided into departmental compartments. This is not so for the local authority, despite attempts at corporate management. Some of housing departments' problems stem from poor liaison between themselves and the architects or planners, for example. The wrong houses get built in the wrong places. But there are several examples now of architects moving toward participatory design in public housing or rehabilitation.

The Byker Redevelopment Area on Tyneside is an interesting example. It attracted attention as the work of a practice (Ralph Erskine's) which was professionally well known and unusually attuned to the social implications of architecture. The objectives were to rehouse existing residents without breaking family ties, patterns of life or valued associations. The office for the job was set up in a corner-shop in the middle of Byker. The architects hoped to get to know first hand the users of their designs, to demystify the architects' role and to give the local authority a defined physical point of entry into the area. They did not call what they were attempting 'participation'. They saw it as a matter of talking to the users, to improve designs and help the community cope with its future. Their stumbling block was the local authority rather than the local people. They had to exert considerable persuasion to have the housing department permit the advance allocation of new housing, which they saw as a solution to residents' anxieties over demolition and redevelopment. But they failed to have alternative forms of tenancy introduced. Ultimately, the architects' problem (and they were not the local authority architects department) was that, while they could enable the users of the new Byker to help in the development of design, it was the local authority which was the client. An independent study (Malpass 1976) of the exercise concluded that participation in Byker failed because the Council insisted on taking the lead and did not give local people a decisive voice in their area. It preferred to seek a consensus rather than allow differences of opinion and conflicts to be disclosed.

In the fields of planning and transportation the alleged 'unrepresentative' nature of participants, particularly of groups or group representatives, led many authorities to adopt survey approaches to the general public. A similar move has been made in housing, though with a different emphasis. In 1972 the Greater London Council and the Department of the Environment jointly began to develop a 'housing appraisal kit', to be generally available to public housing authorities (Burbidge 1975; Francklow 1979). It is a feedback service, based on residents' answers to a questionnaire. It is intended to 'assist . . . in matching designs more closely to the needs of inhabitants, in identifying and avoiding repeating the mistakes of the past and wherever possible in improving existing schemes'. As we suggested in an earlier chapter, market research is not participation; it is diverting the ideology to consumerism.

A group of architects who have been active in participatory housing for more than ten years is the ASSIST team in Glasgow (Thornley 1977). They were initially stimulated by the Corporation's wish to municipalise and improve tenement buildings, and in the process to rehouse their residents. They believed that it should be the residents who had control of their local environment and that individuals should have a say in deciding what improvements would be made to their houses and when. In the early 1970s ASSIST architects were successful, through the medium of housing associations, in enabling hundreds of owners and tenants to improve their tenement dwellings in a modest, affordable and personally acceptable way.

The improvement of tenement property is an interesting context for participation. Tenements are three or four-storey buildings with a common entrance and two or three houses (flats) on each floor. Most are of mixed tenure, owner-occupied and rented. The roof, stairs, foundations and fabric of the building are owned jointly between all the houses. The most important improvements needed were new kitchens and bathrooms. To achieve this residents on lower floors had to agree to pipes passing through their house, even if they did not wish for improvements themselves. In a number of ways individuals were forced to recognise that the exercise was a co-operative venture, and groups of residents also had to recognise the rights of individuals. The relation between the individual and the group was sufficiently important for one member of ASSIST to describe the exercise as a good 'educative vehicle for democratisation'.

The local people also learned to work with the local authority. The authority's methods of house improvement were not working, but it was willing to help the residents' groups and housing associations which local organisations already in existence set up as a base for action. However the circumstances were unusual. The established institutions which might have provided barriers were in a state of uncertainty and change, in anticipation of the 1975 local government reorganisation. The impression is not given that similar relationships could arise in any other circumstances.

Although some participatory benefits did emerge, there was no noticeable redistribution of resources as a result. The shifts of power which occurred were in some ways questionable. Some control of affairs passed from the local authority to the housing associations; but the latter were formally less democratic institutions. Overall power over housing of this type became centralised with the Housing Corporation, a non-elected body.

ASSIST itself became more professionalised during the 1970s, with a staff hierarchy and unionisation providing further impediments to flexibility. In the early years ASSIST had combined the roles of architect, community worker and broker; and admitted that sometimes the members went against the rules of the architectural profession. Later they left many of their tasks to community workers and concentrated on architecture. The design and the product improved, but at the expense of innovation and a full relationship with the residents who were the clients. Instead staff found themselves working for an increasingly conventional, professionalised housing association committee. More recently, ASSIST has tried to break free by launching a scheme to help owner-occupiers keep clear of housing associations and improve their property without professional help.

Housing associations and co-operatives were intended in part to be a solution to the bureaucratic control and intricacies of subsidy which have dogged the post-war history of housing. In turn they are overtaken by the same maladies. A more radical solution has been insufficiently tried so far to know whether it will go the same way. 'Self-build' is not uncommon in Scandinavia and the USA. But in Britain a combination of rigid design and construction restrictions, as well as difficulties with funding economical self-build types such as timber-frame houses, has made the option rare.

A pilot scheme was recently started by Lewisham Borough Council, with Walter Segal, a long-term advocate of the method (McKean 1976). He believes that if the barriers can be removed, it offers the potential to speed up housing completions, shorten waiting lists and produce more humane architecture. In particular, detached houses for small families can be built for as little as one-third of the cost of a similar conventional dwelling, using the family's own management and labour resources. Self-build can be done by the individual, particularly if a low technology programme is used. One or two co-operative schemes which relied on traditional building methods and the shared, skilled and unskilled labour of their members have run into difficulties over group frictions. Union protests also have to be met. But local authorities are in a strong position to promote such schemes if they have the will. Both the land and the financing are at their disposal; and they can exercise discretion over construction and design controls. To do so would involve a further shift from being providers and controllers to being enablers; and success would depend partly on the authority conceding that people have managerial as well as manual skills. A community's experience of having co-operated in raising their homes from the ground should be a firm basis for a continuing participatory life together. This would be one rather special way for a local authority to achieve the aim expressed forty years ago by the Central Housing Advisory Committee (CHAC 1938), that good housing management should be a form of social education, 'teaching a new and inexperienced community to be housing minded'.

Chapter seven

LOCAL HEALTH SERVICES

In formal organisational terms this chapter is somewhat anomalous. It deals with a service which is not now provided locally through the local government system. Rather it enjoys its own separate forms of local organisation which have evolved, not without argument, over the century and a half of state involvement in health care. The emergence of this entirely separate organisation has not been entirely the result of concern for public participation in, and control of, health services. But that has been one of the recurrent themes in the debate over structure and organisation and gives the service special significance for us.

In the mid-nineteenth-century period of initial state involvement with public health, a key debate hinged around whether control of any state service should be vested in central hands or remain with 'local governments'. Underlying that debate was the argument that local control was desirable because it ensured greater responsiveness and accountability to the local population. This was matched by a centralising argument in terms of wider public interests than the merely local and in terms of equity considerations between different localities. The issue was not resolved then. The mainly environmental health concerns of the period were sometimes taken up by the post-1835 Municipal Corporations and sometimes by *ad hoc* local health boards, both watched over by a central board. From our perspective these are interesting beginnings though one would not expect much public participation at that stage. The state of the franchise, nationally and locally, gave little credence to the claims for democracy at either level. Other forms of participation were at best limited to a narrow élite.

By the turn of the century state involvement in health services had developed considerably, but the issue of control and organisation of the service remained. National and local government had

Local health services

both become more representative, at least in the formal sense, and had both become involved in a much wider range of public services. At the same time notions of public health had developed and the earlier environmental preoccupations had given rise to a concern with hospital provision and with primary care through the general practitioner. Environmental health had become a local government service, while hospitals were provided by Poor Law Guardians, by charitable organisations, by local authorities and privately. General practice was the main focus of debate as Lloyd George's national health insurance sought to widen its availability. In the event the Act of 1911 created *ad hoc* local committees thereby forestalling local government control. This appeased medical interests and those of the private insurance companies, though it also isolated the service from public involvement. Overall the health service became highly fragmented with general practitioners most clearly immunised from democratic control.

Much more profound than either of those two earlier debates was the lengthy discussion over the possible introduction of a national health service in the 1940s. The legacy of fragmentation and varied local control had produced a wide variety of provision, particularly in relation to general practice and hospital care. The service could not cope with the pressures of war-time demand and the emergency medical services revealed traditional weaknesses and paved the way for thoroughgoing reform. Various suggestions were canvassed. Local authorities already provided hospital care, environmental protection, and a range of domiciliary services and one obvious proposal was that they should take over a national health service. This would have secured direct democratic control. The strong professional opposition to such a possibility was clearly articulated and the ultimate ministerial rejection of the proposal reflected a wish to conciliate medical opinion.

In the event the solution adopted and implemented in 1948 maintained separate organisations for running hospitals, general practice and community services. Such fragmentation did much to secure the traditional professional dominance of major aspects of health care. General practice remained separate under the control locally of non-elected Executive Councils. Local government retained its mixture of environmental and domiciliary services. At the same time it lost its control over hospitals which were brought together under non-elected Regional Boards and Hospital Management Committees. Each of these purely health service organisations involved substantial direct professional participation, in sharp contrast to local government which debarred employees from serving on their employing council as elected members. Wider public representation was sought entirely through the device of local government nomination to reserved places. Given our earlier comments on local government itself, it seems certain that this device would not secure any effective indirect public participation. Health issues would hardly be relevant to a local government elector already concerned about a wide range of local authority services.

Similar debates arose during the years before the reorganisation of 1974 which introduced the current structure. Once again the merits of direct local government control were put forward and once again they were dismissed. Indeed the ultimate reorganisation removed services from local government control in seeking to bring all the health services under the control of one authority. Involvement by elected local government would be secured by creating uniform boundaries for both authorities and developing effective liaison arrangements. General practice was again kept separate but other health services were organised under Regional and Area Health Authorities, neither to be directly elected. Instead, once again, professional representation was secured, local authorities were to nominate members and the Minister also to fill some places. The justification for this structure was the need for more effective management of the health services and it was recognised that it left a gap in terms of representation and participation of the public in the running of this major service.

Steps were taken to fill that gap. A Health Service Commissioner was appointed to provide a channel for individuals to air their grievances about the health service in the same way as the Parliamentary Commissioner and the Local Government Commissioner. At the same time Community Health Councils were created to represent local interests in the running of the health service. More will be said about each of these developments later. For the moment it is sufficient to observe that they represent a move to balance the dominant professional interest in the basic structure of health administration with some public representation.

Not that the 1974 reorganisation settled any of these issues for very long. As early as May 1976 a Royal Commission was appointed to consider 'in the interests both of the patients and of those who work in the National Health Service the best use and management of the financial and manpower resources' of the service (Royal Commission 1979). Among other things considered was the question of local government control of health services, receiving 'evidence' from the local government associations that 'the most crucial decision before the Commission is whether the service will be returned to the public. Such a step, with the agreement of the professions, would go a long way to ensure a Health Service which belongs locally and to which people feel committed' (Royal Commission 1979: para. 6, 18). Without very obviously considering the justification for such a claim on behalf of local government, the Commission decided against any change of control. It was well aware of the professional opposition to any such move and the difficulties which any change of control would bring.

This long-standing debate about the structure and organisation of the health service with its implicit concern with democracy and participation, and its ultimate separation from local government, make it interesting to compare with other local services. But they are not the only differences between health and those other services. Indeed health is not a singular service as its fragmented history and organisation demonstrates. Public health was the first aspect of health care to engage the attention of the state, and for obvious reasons. Industrialisation and urbanisation brought exaggerated problems of ill-health and a growing recognition that environmental factors such as housing, drainage, sewerage and water supply caused many of those problems. Inevitably they affect everyone in a local area requiring collective action if they are to be dealt with effectively. But if public health must be universal in its application and so justifies state intervention, there remains a problem about who should decide such universal questions. This was complicated in the nineteenth century because there was no consensus about the relationship between environment and disease. In addition, any cures were expensive and the costs of any action affected different people in different ways. Public health may produce universal benefits, but its costs are by no means so universal. Such problems were further reinforced when public health tackled problems of housing, property-owning interests resenting any compulsion applied to landlords. Much of the public debate is now resolved, though there are still issues of housing and clean air or pollution which raise these sort of conflicts.

At the other end of the spectrum of health care are a range of primary medical and associated domiciliary services which cater for specific individuals, usually in circumstances which do not affect the wider community. In this they are closely analagous with the personal social services. Inevitably these are labour intensive services provided by a wide range of different staff. At one extreme are general medical practitioners with their powerful professional organisations and considerable influence as we have already seen. At the other are home helps who lack both of those characteristics. More importantly, primary medical care is unlike other health services and social services in having an almost universal clientele. Almost all of us register with a general practitioner, and almost certainly use his services at some time. Domiciliary services are more restricted, health visitors to young families and home helps to the elderly. This means that we all have an interest in the quality of primary medical care though with little sense of any continuity of interest or of shared interest with other users. We are free and able to change our doctor if we are dissatisfied and can, in principle, negotiate the quality of service we receive. This very individualised character of primary medicine distinguishes it from other health care, and is reflected in its special and separate organisation.

Hospital care falls somewhere between public health and primary medicine in terms of these particular aspects. Hospitals are a collective form of service in the sense that single institutions serve particular catchment areas, leaving the patient little choice about where to attend for treatment. Recent decisions to concentrate hospital resources confirm this factor and the opposition to consequent hospital closures reflects public recognition of the value of a local service. At the same time hospitals offer labour intensive services. The quality of medical, nursing and ancillary staff determines the quality of care, and recent disputes illustrate the vital role played by menial staff in maintaining the hospital service. Inevitably the hospital service combines the issues peculiar to both public health and primary medicine. Hospital building generates widespread concern as the siting of new, secure mental hospitals illustrates. Similarly hospital closures arouse vocal, and sometimes successful, opposition. At the same time within any given hospital setting, the number and quality of staff, and consequent treatment, can vary considerably. The care a patient receives is almost as much a matter of patient–doctor interaction as is the case in general practice. Again as with general practice most of us experience hospital treatment at some time, though it is unpredictable in its incidence, and usually less frequent than contact with a general practitioner. The exception to this rule are the chronic sick whose concern for, and involvement with, medical services is quite distinct from that of the normal member of the population.

What might all this mean for participation? Formally we have seen that the health services at the local level are organised to give extensive professional involvement and limited public participation. This reflects the powerful position enjoyed by organised medicine throughout the development of state health provision and the weakness of any base for public participation. Different aspects of health care seem to offer different potential for public involvement. There are obvious points at which a collective interest would be relevant and might manifest itself. Equally there are numerous cases where the issues are about individual care or treatment and where the issues are much more about consumerism than about participation.

INDIVIDUAL PARTICIPATION

At the level of service to the individual patient a number of points should be made. First, it must be noted that the take-up of health care is almost always voluntary. There is no compulsion to go to the doctor, to enter hospital or to have treatment, though the hallmark of traditional public health programmes was that individuals had no such choice. But voluntary take-up does not mean that we avoid paying for the service. Since the nineteenth century much individual health care has been offered free to the actual patient, and been paid for out of general tax revenue, in spite of a nominal insurance basis to the service. Charges have been made for various services, but they do not alter the general picture of universal concern with the costs of the service, matched by partial and periodic consumption. In short there is a case for all of us to be concerned with health care services, though our interests often lie in seeing them reduced in order to save costs.

One implication of the voluntary character of health care is that many people do participate, principally by withdrawing from the service or at least not entering it. Individually such non-participation is an interesting phenomenon, but collectively its implications are profound. Despite its ever increasing cost this phenomenon does make the service cheaper than it would otherwise be, though this is not the motive for withdrawal. In addition the pattern of non-use probably subsumes two kinds of people. The poor are clearly less frequent users, sometimes because the services available to them are inadequate, sometimes out of ignorance or indifference. The rich too may also be less frequent users, opting for private medical services rather than accept the limitations of state service. This group have the additional effect of removing an important voice from the debate about health care. In most service settings they would be the group most likely to participate, and the existence of alternative services allows them to vote with their feet by opting out (Hirschman 1970). Participation by such groups in the health service debate, it is argued, would improve the overall service, but experience in health and other sectors suggests it would not equalise its distribution (RAWP 1976).

For the bulk of the population who do use the health services two participatory issues are relevant. The first relates to the overall character of the service and its policies and the general relationship which the public enjoys with its decision-makers. The second relates to the individual's personal problems in relation to care and the way in which dissatisfaction and grievance with medical services are handled. These two elements are of course connected. Changes in the former could well give rise to much reduced concern with particular individual problems. Conversely, preoccupation with individual problems can all too easily distract people from the wider concerns of policy and practice. But however closely related in practice the two are seldom linked institutionally or in debate about the service.

The nature of most modern health services then is closely akin to the personal social services and has very similar features in relation to access to services, and the quality of service secured. The labour intensive nature of most health services, and the professional status of the central workers involved, together limit the scope available to the patient. The type and style of care are determined by professional staff and so too are eligibility for such treatment and access to it. As we have remarked, many people secure their autonomy by opting not to seek medical treatment, but those who do attend the doctor also surrender their autonomy. At least that is true for the clinical aspects of health care. In some cases that clinical judgement may be conditioned by resource availability or bed space or other factors which are a product of separate decisions. Administrative and political decisions can and do influence clinical judgements and yet are an aspect of health care which falls outside the normal individual involvement. The patient often blames the doctor when he had little choice about the treatment available. More importantly for us, the patient participates very little in those other decision areas. He is largely a helpless victim whether it be of clinical, administrative or political decisions.

Local health services

INSTITUTIONAL PARTICIPATION: THE PARLIAMENTARY
COMMISSIONER

Institutionally this situation has been partly recognised although it
required a number of acute cases of unsatisfactory individual treatment to stimulate action. The introduction of the Parliamentary
Commissioner (or Ombudsman) in 1967 to investigate claims of
general maladministration prompted discussion as to whether the
health services might have a similar appointment. Advocates of
such a development were reinforced by a number of scandals within the health service, particularly cases of mistreatment of patients
within long-stay mental hospitals. The decision to reorganise the
National Health Service structure in 1974 provided an opportunity
to effect other changes and the Health Service Commissioner was
appointed in that year. From our perspective several important
points need to be made about this development.

First, it performs the valuable role of ventilating grievances, but
of course this is retrospective in its operation. The impact on recurrent practice of such investigation, despite the clarity of many reports, must be doubted. Second, the legislation limited the sphere
of operation of the Commissioner by excluding the doctor's clinical
judgement from his remit. Some indication of the significance of
this omission may be gauged from early figures of cases referred to
the Commissioner. In the first full year of operation, 1974–75,
there were 612 complaints received of which 354 were outside the
Commissioner's terms of reference. Of that 354 about one-sixth
were concerned with issues of clinical judgement (Stacey 1978).
Third, and most importantly so far as the issue of participation is
concerned, the ombudsman system normally limits complaints to
the individual level, though the health service has gone further
than the more general Parliamentary Commissioner in providing
wider capacity. The Health Service Commissioner is allowed to
take up cases where 'there is an alleged failure in a service' or an
'alleged failure to provide a service'. These clauses widen the notion of grievance and allow the system to be used to raise what are
much more obviously policy questions. These wider matters are
about the level of service and about its distribution, not merely
about individual access or treatment.

These rather critical comments are not intended as an argument
against the appointment of a Commissioner. Individual grievances
are important and can, in the aggregate, produce policy changes.
Indeed pressure groups in other fields (the Child Poverty Action

Group in relation to Social Security) have tried to use test cases, or the statistics of a range of cases, as the basis for a campaign to change the general rules of access or the policy of provision. But it is difficult to make this shift in the level of focus. By their nature individual grievance procedures tend to reinforce existing practices. They give the individual an outlet which limits the pressure for more general change. Not that all individuals use such channels. Like so many aspects of what might be called the consumer movement, they provide a channel for those capable of using it. That invariably means the middle class. That aspect is heavily reinforced by the fact that the Commissioner may only take cases when the complainant has already taken his complaint through the normal health service channels. The capacity and tenacity to do that, and then approach the Commissioner, are not widespread.

INSTITUTIONAL PARTICIPATION: THE COMMUNITY HEALTH COUNCILS

The other institutional innovation of the 1974 reorganisation comes nearer to what we consider to be participation, in theory at least. The Community Health Council was introduced in part to compensate for the absence of any direct democracy within the management system of the National Health Service locally. This in turn reflected the view that management could be segregated from popular representation, and indeed that it should be. This perhaps reflects a rather simplistic view of the nature of management and the degree to which decisions can be treated in such a pure fashion. Management and policy run very close in the public sector and the Bains' view of their relationship in local government might have provided a better model for the health services (Bains 1972). In fact the Labour party argued such a view, preferring the model of local government as a basis of organisation, although it must be said that our own analysis does not suggest that that is perfect either. In any event the new Community Health Councils reflect an official acceptance of the need for a public voice. Whether the form of Community Health Council adopted is a workable form of participation, and if it is, whether it is better than direct representation are questions which must be considered later.

In looking for answers two elements might be considered. One involves the basis of membership of the Community Health Council and the relationship which it has with its community. The other concerns the activity of the Community Health Council and how it relates to the National Health Service and the quality of local services. Both are important and obviously closely interrelated.

The first of these would have been easier to judge if the Councils had been directly elected, even though local government illustrates that that is no guarantee of representativeness or responsiveness. But they are not elected. They are nominated, one-half from the local authority, one-third from voluntary organisations and one-sixth by the Regional Health Authority. Even that composition required effective parliamentary debate as the original proposals would have secured even greater numbers from within the health service, 50 per cent to be nominated by the Area Health Authority. The composition finally agreed secures some independence for the Community Health Council, but hardly goes far to secure representation for the local community. The local authority nominees could be argued to afford tenuous formal representative links, but local elections are not strongly locally determined, and certainly not concerned with local health matters. Councillors do meet constituents in their local authority work and could tap opinions about health services, but it is doubtful if they do. Voluntary organisation representatives may or may not be representative of the local population, though most writing about such groups suggests that they represent only certain sections of the people. Equally they may or may not be concerned as groups with health services and consequently knowledgeable and aware. Attempts have been made by central government to encourage such relevant choices, though the mechanisms for locating and securing such representatives are not obvious. Nor is it necessarily good to recruit such expertise. The role of the Community Health Council may be better seen as communicating lay opinion, and as we shall see, many of the groups concerned with health care already have assumed strong 'professional' characteristics.

In fact the operation and outcome of the nomination system reveals the same situation as applies to so many attempts to encourage participation. In a recent study of Local Health Councils, the Scottish equivalent, Bochel and MacLaran (1979: 452) examined various notions of representation. Specifically they examined three interpretations of representation: '(1) representation in a microcosmic sense; (2) representation in the sense of being a cross-section of interests; (3) representation through an élite which possesses certain qualifications specifically: (a) experience, special knowledge and common sense; (b) a wide range of contacts.' Their survey reinforced earlier findings on English councils in that they were 'extremely unrepresentative of the community at large' and 'over-whelmingly middle-class and middle-aged in composition' (Bochel and MacLaran 1979: 454). This is not surprising and reflects findings about most other forms of participation, both elected and non-elected. It does, however, raise questions about the legitimacy of Community Health Councils as well as reflecting a failure on the part of government to give serious thought to how to secure effective representation. As Bochel and MacLaran remark 'microcosmic criteria were never thought through in the setting-up process, and no real attempt has been made to produce a body representative in that sense' (Bochel and MacLaran 1979: 456).

The same criticism may be applied to Community Health Councils in other interpretations of representation. Representation of interests through voluntary group nominations is limited by several factors. In many cases the initiators of group nominations come from within the National Health Service and their knowledge is limited to the well known or those already concerned with health care services in some way, a situation much like that in some cases of public participation in planning (Boaden and Collins 1975). Further selectivity occurs because many groups are middle class in membership and élitist in their organisation, both of which limit this method of securing community participation. And even if such problems can be overcome there remain large numbers of non-joiners who fall outside the representative structure organised in this way. Those whose interests fail to get heard are every bit as important as those who are heard. In short there are serious deficiencies among Health Councils in terms of representation with a consequent weakening of their legitimacy, which is in any case questioned by some within the health services. There may be a tendency as a result for them to seek legitimacy through expertise rather than through representation, a not uncommon way to seek influence from outside the formal service organisation. This would seem likely to produce a pattern either of co-optation (the insider outsider) or of weakness because issues are defined in agreed service terms. It may be that examination of what Health Councils have done will throw further light on this.

To anyone familiar with participation in planning and its statutory shape, it will come as little surprise that the formal terms of reference of Health Councils are either opaque or all-embracing. Formally the Act requires the Council to 'represent the interests in the National Health Service of the public in its district' (NHS Act 1973) which does not take one very far. Subsequent advice from

Government to Councils went to the other extreme with shopping lists of matters with which they might want to become involved. Distinct from what they might want to do but influencing their choice, Councils enjoy certain rights in relation to the Health Service. On the basis that their command over information must be a crucial weapon in their armoury they are entitled to receive information from their Area Health Authority and must be consulted on key matters like hospital closures. Whilst information is a key resource there are dangers in this situation within the Health Service. Because the operational authorities are not representative in intention, there is a danger that the Community Health Council will become an arm of the system, diffusing information through the community and acting close to the role of public relations agent for the Area Health Authority. Another problem is that the gathering of information becomes a dominant and totally absorbing task, certainly for organisations with usually only one full-time worker. Inevitably if they are not careful information systems can become so dense (after all the National Health Service is large and complex) that the Council will not be able to see the wood for the trees. These are obvious dangers for the Councils, and they must be reconciled with the fact that information must often be the trigger to action, and may be the key to success.

Important rights are also secured to Health Councils to be consulted by Area Health Authorities about their plans, and particularly about key decisions to open new facilities or close old ones. These are vital elements in consideration of local health care, but while Councils must be concerned with them there are again attendant dangers, particularly for such new organisations. Health care planning, like structure planning which we have considered elsewhere (Boaden *et al* 1980), is complex, long term and invariably involves technical considerations unfamiliar to laymen. These elements present obvious problems in terms of participation, and probably encourage the adoption of professional roles by Council members which can lead to obvious forms of co-option. All of these tendencies are likely to distance Councils from their communities. New facilities and closures are easier to focus and understand, but present other problems. Given the large scale of each Community Health Council area (there are only 225 in all) both kinds of issue are likely to have variable effects within the area of a single Council. New facilities, if there are to be any, raise obvious locational and distributional questions. If it is a clinic to be sited there may be keen competition assuming alternative sites are available. If it is a

secure mental hospital most people may simply want it, but somewhere else. At this point the Community Health Council may seek
to resolve such problems creating obvious tensions internally, and
equally obvious benefits to the Area Health Authority. Closures are
easier in the sense that they secure much greater local consensus,
but they generate other difficulties. They inevitably absorb large
amounts of Council resources as they have to be fought intensely
when they arise. This may produce success, but it can be bought at
the expense of other issues, relevant to other areas, and possibly
every bit as significant. Inevitably Community Health Councils face
serious difficulties in setting priorities within their work and making the best use of their limited resources. Their powers and the
nature of their membership go a long way towards explaining their
choice of action. The precise degree of participation inherent in
their choices is more difficult to assess.

Understandably there is a wide variety of experience among
Community Health Councils. They are new organisations, born
when the Health Service was undergoing profound changes, and
they face quite varied local health services, populations and problems. Yet some common themes do appear, at least in their earlier
years of operation. One theme is action to assist complainants
against the service. This was an obvious corollary of the features of
the complaints system and the complexity of the health services
which have already been considered. Without disparaging such
activity it necessarily falls short of their intended collective role,
and does not appear to have very marked impact on the provision
of health care. Like other agencies who develop such advocacy services there is a tendency for them to become dominant in the overall work. It is difficult to turn people away; success in such work
breeds its own increased demand for help; it also produces a threa-
tening image of the Council within the Health Service which may
inhibit other more co-operative action. At the same time it fulfils a
valuable service and provides useful links with some people in the
community as well as offering work which volunteers can undertake. Once again the Council has a delicate position to maintain if it
is to engage the range of possible functions it might perform.

Another common activity is the conduct of surveys of local opinion about the National Health Service, and surveys of the actual
provision made. In part, the former serve a useful purpose in re-
vealing community attitudes in a way not otherwise available to
rather unrepresentative bodies. At the same time they are a rather
blunt instrument for doing this and may have other disadvantages

(Boaden and Walker 1976). As Klein and Lewis observe 'How are they [CHC Members] to react if their own personal priorities ... come into conflict with the priorities of the populations whom they represent?' (Klein and Lewis 1976: 121). Obviously this is a difficult area made more so by the fact that surveys misleadingly produce quantified and precise information which does not often engage the full complexity of health care decisions. The expertise of the Council can be set against the views of the people. Like any other representative institution the problem is whether to follow or to lead local opinion. The theory of our representative system suggests that Council members should not be mere delegates, but the implications of taking a different line have to be borne in mind. Certainly they ought to be explained to the public more fully than is the case now. If your only role is to complete a questionnaire which is then ignored few can complain about resultant apathy.

If there are potential conflicts between different publics and between Council members and those publics, there are also problems in the relationship between the Council and professional health service interests. Inevitably perhaps, having segregated management from representation, there will be Council criticism of staff within the service. Klein and Lewis cite an example of such conflict in relation to obstetric care and induced labour in childbirth (Klein and Lewis 1976). In their case, and it is surely not isolated, the reaction of the consultant was to reaffirm the protected nature of the clinical decision and to impose on the Health Council the same limitation as was successfully imposed on the Health Commissioner. Nor is it only the medical staff who seek immunity from such external pressure. Other staff within the service were equally firm that limits must be set to what Health Councils could take up. There are some signs that this opposition may be giving way to more co-operative views in face of the present cutbacks in service. On the overall issue of levels of spending, community and professionals are at one in seeking increased spending, or inhibiting reductions. When the debate is about how such resources are used, where and on what specialisms, the unanimity dissolves and the autonomy of the professional is reasserted.

This critical relationship with the professionals must be seen in relation to the common Health Council activity of securing member involvement in other parts of the Health Service machinery. As the Royal Commission observes most are represented in some way on National Health Service planning teams, about one-third attended joint consultative meetings, and the reasonable figure of one-quarter had secured attendance at Family Practitioner Committee meetings where they have no rights of access and where professional autonomy is most heavily guarded (Royal Commission 1979). All of this may inhibit the conflicts just discussed and may also facilitate the flow of information central to any present or future campaigning. It clearly opens up channels of communication, though the price of using them may be dilution of some of the messages being delivered. It is doubtful whether such attendance and contact have yet produced much real effect on health service decisions. Chris Ham has offered 'one generalisation that is unfair to some, but, I think, justified by many, that on the whole councils have been far too polite and deferential' (Barnard and Lee 1977: 104). If that is the price of negotiated attendance it may be too high. If it is a reflection of the attitudes of members of Councils, then that may need to change.

Of course it may simply stem from the fact that Community Health Councils have been accorded statutory status. As with planning, such statutorily required participation may be a two-edged sword. Statutory status gives added weight to participation especially where, as here, it has clear institutional shape. At the same time, such institutions must behave 'responsibly' and may be used to justify limited access by other non-statutory external bodies. The Community Health Council becomes the 'legitimate' voice of the consumer. Other voices need not be heard and can now be rejected on grounds of unrepresentativeness. Or it may be that Councils have not yet been long enough established to have achieved that position. Health service administrators certainly do not yet seem to accept them as quite so strongly institutionalised. It may be better if they do not become so. W.J.M. Mackenzie's view should lend some caution to development: 'Personally, I believe more has been done, and can be done, by a voluntary movement of quite a different kind, which has no statutory basis and has only recently attracted attention both in the United Kingdom and in the United States' (Mackenzie 1979: 45). That other voluntary movement deserves some consideration here.

VOLUNTARY GROUPS IN THE HEALTH SERVICE

Professor Mackenzie's view will be shared by many who repose great faith in the potential of the 'voluntary sector' for securing public participation, though he is not using that expression in the same way that we are. Indeed his own large range of examples indicate that the voluntary movement is diverse even within the health services. Some organisations do see their role as to push for improvements in the health services, and for greater public participation in decision-making. The Patients' Association perhaps typifies this stance, though as its name implies, it sees the public primarily being involved as patients. There is little of the radical flavour which sees public services like health as a legitimate area for popular control. Other organisations are much more concerned with their members' interests, often narrowly conceived. Some like Mencap and Age Concern do press for improvement in services in mental care and care of the elderly. Others like the Psoriasis Association and the Colostomy Welfare Group are more concerned to provide mutual self-help, a category of activity which is enjoying a revival. Partly that reflects failures in the statutory services, and partly the very different motivation which sees self-help as a way of saving resources in the public services. In short the voluntary movement in health care is as varied as in any other area of service.

Voluntary group activity is seen as a hopeful area for public participation by those who take a pluralist view of our polity and who see the interplay of group interests as the basis of decision-making. A recent commentary from that perspective considers three major organisations. Age Concern and MIND typify the national pressure group in this context. They both started out providing services to the elderly and mentally handicapped, respectively. Over time the improvement in government services to both groups has allowed them, and in part forced them, to turn into pressure groups for improved government service. They cannot compete with public services, and filling gaps left by them is often not satisfactory. More than that, they cannot accept the limitations on government services. Consequently they become national lobbyists, often in part funded by government. Their success is limited, however, and examination of any recent studies of either sector must cause one to question their effectiveness. If the plural model works it does so imperfectly.

The Patients' Association is rather different. It was founded only in 1963 to represent the interests of patients as a whole. Its origins stem from much the same concerns that gave rise finally to the appointment of a Health Service Commissioner. Inevitably its early emphases lay with individual grievances and how these might be dealt with most effectively. Many groups have made the move from there to more general concerns (Shelter and CPAG come readily to mind) but within the health services context it is hard to disagree with Professor Mackenzie who observes 'a very gallant attempt to found a general Patient's Association has not been heard of much recently' (Mackenzie 1979: 45).

There are several issues here which merit consideration. There is obviously increasing voluntary activity of one sort or another. Much of it is designed to give necessary mutual support to people suffering from disease or disability (Psoriasis and Huntington's Chorea are two examples), both of which can produce stigma and isolation for sufferers. Such activity, though worth while, has little direct effect on the statutory services. If anything it serves to reduce the effects in certain fields of both their inadequacy and their style. This in its turn is reinforced by a dual tendency among such groups. On the one hand they tend to adopt similar views about illness and its cause as those adopted by health service professionals. On the other hand they have to resort to professional and bureacratic tendencies in maintaining their own organisations in being (Robinson and Henry 1977). Of course they do a great deal of good for their members, but in the wider sense Robinson and Henry's conclusion seems inevitable: 'It does not take long to realise that, for a variety of reasons, self-help groups seem neither inclined, nor likely to be able, to accomplish any grand political changes (Robinson and Henry 1977: 125). A similar conclusion about other groups seems equally safe, though their potential for gaining and using power and for achieving particular and limited reforms may be quite high.

One does not have to seek far for possible explanations for this relative weakness. Some of the medical conditions with which people organise to cope are stigmatising and consequently isolating. The individual overcomes his isolation by joining the group, but often that is sufficient and the group prefers to remain isolated in its collective strength. For the more acute and episodic health conditions it is hardly rational for the individual to organise. If care is bad or inadequate, he may seek redress after the event, hopefully not too late. The condition will probably not recur and insurance against future need may be more rationally engaged through BUPA than through organisation. More importantly, the acute episode is the one where the patient is most dependent on the professional and therefore least willing to challenge professional autonomy. If patient autonomy has to be traded for skilled care, most of us would opt for the latter. It may be a pity that such choices are necessary, but they are.

Another factor is that the disease base of organisations, like that of organised medical care, produces excessive fragmentation. This makes it difficult to produce any concerted general pressure, even when the issues at stake do affect most organisations in the same way. All may share a common concern at their own weakness *vis-à-vis* professionals, but never come together to attack that issue. At the same time, the fact that their organisation mirrors that of the service can produce too much sharing with the particular professional group. Robinson and Henry observe in their study that the professional often plays a key role in stimulating, managing and encouraging self-help groups, which in turn must reinforce the tendency for them not to be too critical (Robinson and Henry 1977.) Even Mackenzie is cautious about the prospects for concerted group pressure: 'patients' associations have hardly recognised themselves yet as fragments of a single movement' (Mackenzie 1979: 49). That may reflect the dominance of particular interests but it must also raise doubts about the prospective impact of such organisations.

It is worth adding here that some of these problems also apply to organisations formed on a geographical rather than a disease or specialism base. This issue of 'community' as a base of organisation is dealt with in Chapter 3, and as we saw, Community Health Councils face problems in seeking to represent geographical constituencies. The recent debate on National Health Service organisation has confirmed a belief in the need for such Councils to represent smaller areas. Yet as we have said, they are not really small enough to ensure consensus. The result is again divisive. Until such time as clearer collective interests emerge it seems probable that public involvement will remain weak and relatively ineffectual. Only when a more adequate base is provided for public participation will it do much to influence the divisions and inadequacies within the management of the National Health Service.

Chapter eight

SOCIAL SERVICES

The personal social services differ in several ways from the other local government services we are considering although there are some similarities to education. In this chapter we shall concentrate on two of these aspects of social services which have implications for the development of public participation. First, there is the notion of dependency. Most people who approach the personal social services, or who are approached by them, are in need of help of some kind. They are unable to solve the problems of their immediate or particular social situation for themselves, they are in the position of supplicants. Second, there is the involvement of many voluntary agencies in the provision of personal welfare and social services. This is more common than in other services, and its voluntary character changes the nature of the statutory/non-statutory relationship when compared with private schools for example, or with private housing. In personal social services there is an element of partnership rather than a division into distinct sectors of provision.

The personal social services range extensively in the tasks they undertake, from residential care for the elderly and children to case-work services for individual clients, from providing direct financial help in a small number of cases to giving practical assistance in many more. They provide services in people's homes such as home help, meals on wheels, or the installation of telephones for the isolated and housebound. In addition, staff intercede on behalf of clients with other local government departments, with central government and with private or voluntary organisations. This great diversity has emerged over a long period with varying trends occurring at different times. Many of the individual services emerged at times when participation was not in vogue. Indeed, in some cases, they arose from Poor Law services receipt of which led to the forfeiting of citizen rights and certainly not to participation. Other services grew out of the work of the early Charity Organisation Society with its emphasis on deservingness and its stigmatising investigation of eligibility for help among clients. Those qualities have disappeared or diminished over the years, but the character of the clientele and the nature of the service continue to make participation, at least among clients, a difficult proposition.

The early origins of these services are important, but the present provisions effectively date from the codifying period in social welfare after the Second World War. Not that the policies of the late 1940s provided a completely unified system, they did not. The 1948 legislation conferred wide responsibilities on the elected local authorities. Children in need were to be catered for by a separate department with its own committee of councillors. The National Assistance Act conferred responsibilities in respect of the elderly and handicapped. These responsibilities were held by various departments depending on the attitudes and structures of each authority. This patchwork quality to both the services and the structure perhaps reflects the overall status of personal social services at that time. They were not quite an accepted part of the institutional map. Within the services, it is clear that children were the most privileged client group. Their dependence was quite obviously a natural condition for which they could not be held responsible, and public sympathy could readily be invoked for children in need. The children's departments became the most important of the various departments concerned with social services. The variations in status of different client groups and the several departments concerned with the provision of services were both important to the development of participation.

Developments since the 1940s have greatly clarified the formal picture, though the relative client pecking order almost certainly remains. Children's departments with their statutory base developed quickly, and the officers in them adopted professional status and ideas. The other less privileged sectors developed more slowly, usually seeking independent departmental status as the avenue to staff and service development and to political recognition. By the mid-1960s these developments had gone quite a long way, but new pressures were emerging. Personal social services were widely accepted as part of the welfare state, but views about their character were changing, and the inter-connectedness of social problems and services to meet them was being recognised. The main result was the establishment of a committee to inquire into the Local Authority Social Services under the chairmanship of Lord Seebohm (Seebohm 1968). The committee reported in 1968 and some of its main recommendations were embodied in the Local Authority Social Services Act of 1970.

Chief among those recommendations was the proposal to bring most of the relevant services within one single department. The wide range of services observed at the beginning of this chapter would be carried out by staff working in one department under a single director and with one responsible committee of councillors. One set of arguments in favour of that change had nothing to do with participation directly. They were concerned with efficiency and effectiveness. Merger would give the new department the scale necessary to achieve greater political significance, more viable case-loads for specialist services, and more co-ordinated organisation. These were all features that were reinforced by the wider 1974 reorganisation of local government with its increase in the size of almost all local authorities and consequently of departments. Such changes were expected to bring obvious benefits to clients in terms of coherence of provision, reduction of overlap and clarity of function. They were also expected to enhance the volume of resources provided to personal social services by improving their status and relative bidding power within local government.

The new departments were also argued as having advantages in relation to participation. Creation of a single department would provide a single point of access for the client and render it easier for him or her to know who to approach if he or she needed help. The force of this argument was related to proposed changes in the nature of social work which we shall consider shortly. More importantly the potential for improved opportunities for the clientele could only follow if other aspects of departments were improved. Reception arrangements within social service departments are often not good and can easily undo the advantages of a single point of access (Hall 1974). The enlarged scale of the new departments produces geographical decentralisation which may affect participation in different ways. The fragmentation in departmental administration which it causes can produce varied policies and varied local practices making consistent departmental action difficult. This in turn can make it difficult for those dealing with the department. On the other hand, localisation of service delivery should enhance public awareness and access. If the notions of geographical community that we discuss in Chapter 3 have validity, then local delivery, even where designed for purely administrative reasons, may greatly enhance participation (Abrams 1977).

Several of the other recommendations of the Seebohm Report were relevant to participation, though none lent themselves to enactment in quite the same way as did the recommendations about basic structure. One important recommendation was to change the character of traditional social work from the specialist work with different client groups which had grown out of the fragmented origins of the services. The new generic social workers would see their work as family, rather than client, based and would relate to the family in its community context. The effect of such a change in the character of the work and the profession, and consequently on the position of the client, is not easy to gauge. It might have been expected to reduce the degree of specialist skill of the worker and in so doing enhance the client's relative position. In fact the question is often hypothetical as many departments adapted the proposals and formed generic teams of workers dealing as specialists with their traditional clientele. Whether the client's opportunities are enhanced by access to a team of mixed specialists, or indeed whether he enjoys such access, are difficult questions. Certainly there does not appear to have been any major improvement in this respect and the progress of the social work profession itself suggests that the client position has probably not altered much.

An enhancement of participation might also have been expected from the recommendation of the Seebohm Committee for a stronger role for the community in the determination and provision of social care. There have certainly been developments of this kind, and we will consider some of them below, but they appear largely outside the structure of formal social service provision. As such they are not part of the internal developments which are our immediate concern.

So far we have written about social services as though social workers were their only employees. In fact several groups of workers are employed on a wide range of tasks, and social workers form only a small minority of staff. Residential workers and home helps are numerically dominant and their services command large proportions of social services' budgets. By comparison social workers are small beer. At the same time they represent the élite of the department and come closest to those professional forms and norms which powerfully affect participation. Over recent years social workers have acquired their own professional association complete with a training and accreditation system and code of ethics. As yet not all social workers are qualified, or members of the Association, but the road to a fully qualified profession now looks quite short. The impact of this professional standing on the opportunities for public participation in the service will be considered later.

Non-social-work staff have no comparable professional basis from which to operate. In most cases they perform more routine work and operate within a framework of bureaucratic procedure. Rigid rules about access to material help or the qualifications for receiving home help are cases in point. In residential care admission requirements and the regime after admission are often quite rigid, bearing sometimes close resemblance to their Poor Law forebears. Such rules and procedures can be as inhibiting to outside participants as the expertise and status of professional social workers. Moreover, whatever the implications of either set of working norms and procedures, the presence of both inside a single department make it more difficult for an outsider to comprehend the system and departments themselves may not cope easily with the division.

In addition to the wide range of tasks performed by social service departments there has also been a recent extension of the scope of social work itself. Traditionally the emphasis has been on one-to-one relationships as workers case-work their clients. More recently there has been a growing concern to work with groups of clients and indeed with whole communities. These tendencies were reinforced by the Seebohm Committee recommendations though the techniques themselves are not new. They imply quite different ideas about participation both by clients and by a wider non-client public, and in many cases they also reflect quite different notions about the wider social role of the personal social services. Casework as it emerged from the voluntary work of the Charity Organisation Society involved a pathological view of the origin of social problems and often took a coercive form in relation to client behaviour and obligations (Mowat 1961). The more collective forms of social work start from rather different notions about the origins of social problems. Many problems are seen as being caused by structural factors, both local and national, which affect the clients' situation without their being in any way responsible individually or communally. Such different orientations have implications for participation.

Before looking at some of those implications it is worth reminding ourselves that the participants, or potential participants, in the social services are diverse. There is an obvious democratic role for the public at large, though in general it is felt to be able to exercise it through the conventional representative machinery of local government. In addition there is a critical question about the participation of the clientele, which is echoed in other services such as housing and education. Unusually there is a third category in the case of personal social services. These are the many volunteers who by providing social services themselves obviously influence the statutory services. They have always played this role, but it has become more complex and perhaps more controversial as the State has first accepted a wider role, and then, as now, decided to contract that role. Each of these two latter elements will be considered in turn.

CLIENT PARTICIPATION

Several local authority departments are now considering, or implementing, a degree of client, as distinct from public, participation in the services they provide. Parents and even some pupils are now considered eligible to participate in various school decisions, and council tenants have been given wider rights in the management of their homes. In social services the question of client involvement has a longer pedigree, though this has not produced any obvious greater involvment for clients. Any assessment of their actual involvement must depend on the aspect of social service under review, and on the precise notion of participation being used. To take only the most obvious example: the degree and character of client participation in case-work must be a matter of mutual judgement and inter-personal relationship. The client must have an important role, but it is quite probable that its form is entirely determined by the social worker (Mayer and Timms 1970). In community work it is different. In theory the community is the determining element in the relationship, though it is of course possible for the community worker to play a highly directive role. The emphases between the two types of work are very different and the resources available on each side are also quite distinct.

Case-Work

Looking at the area of case-work more closely the problems of participation are immediately apparent. In the one-to-one relationship between a client and a social worker it is clear that the advantage will normally lie with the latter. He or she is more knowledgeable about the possibilities in any particular situation, more experienced in utilising those opportunities, and almost invariably more articulate. These advantages are enhanced if it becomes necessary to engage third parties to secure some service for the client. It is the worker who will usually do that. All these features must raise questions in any situation in which the social worker and the client disagree, either about the problem or about preferred solutions – the two issues in which the client has a primary interest (Mayer and Timms 1970). Of course clients can, and often do, acquire considerable manipulative skill especially if they have a long 'career' in the social services. Such manipulation almost always consists of the client learning the social worker's rules and playing according to them. This can make the client effective, but it is quite another thing for the client to participate in making the rules. Such wider participation would represent a challenge to the professional norm and is usually rejected on the ground that the individual case should not be allowed to determine general rules. The social worker handles a wide range of cases while the client only experiences his own, and will presumably generalise his own self-interest if allowed to participate more widely. The social worker guards against such a tendency for himself by extensive training and supervision of his practice, as well as by commitment to a professionally prescribed code of ethics.

The recently formulated British Association of Social Workers Code of Ethics is interesting in this context for what it has to say about the 'rights' of the client (BASW 1977). It outlines the rights of clients which workers should observe, and in so doing seeks to defend the autonomy of the professional worker. One basic principle is to 'encourage and facilitate the self-realisation of the individual person' (BASW 1977: 6) which certainly suggests elaborate and effective client participation. This is reinforced by the requirement that 'social workers also have a special responsibility to ensure the fullest possible realisation of his [the applicant's] rights and satisfaction of his needs' (BASW 1977: 9). These are laudable principles but they do not necessarily require a change in the relation between worker and client, rather a heightened concern for the latter on the part of the former. If worker and client disagree about the client's best interests, the ethical code may look strained. The client is unlikely to be able to assert his claim from his relatively weak position and must rely on the social worker's goodwill. The implicit notion of benevolent social work may be rather too simplistic. The function of social work is in part to exercise social control over some of the clientele and this aspect must raise questions about the ethical commitment in the Code.

More favourable to the client, at least in principle, is the recent development of the notion of 'contract' between worker and client as an effective basis for social work. This recognises 'the anxiety resulting from the power imbalance' (between worker and client) (Goldstein 1973: 137) and seeks to establish agreement between both about what each will do during the social work relationship. This is an interesting notion, but the apparent analogy between social work contracts and legal contracts tends not to be present in most cases. John Corden in a stimulating review of this issue stresses that while the legal model may not be the only one which social work could follow, it is a particularly useful model to adopt (Corden 1980). He reviews selected aspects of legal contract 'Offer, Acceptance, Consideration and Intention' (Corden 1980: 146) and illustrates the difficulties in applying them to the very unequal relationship between social worker and client. Despite this he concludes that 'The systematic and explicit use of a contractual model may help to maximize the possibilities of reciprocal relationships' (Corden 1980: 160). That more modest goal is of course desirable in a participatory sense and is happening up to a point. Initial discussions between worker and client are being used to clarify both what the worker can reasonably offer to, and expect from, the client. Communicating in this way clarifies much that was previously not communicated to the client. It does not alter the fact that ultimately there is no redress for the client against the worker, while the latter often retains sanctions over the client. At the end the acute imbalance between worker and client makes contract inappropriate and poses serious problems even for the development of reciprocity.

It is worth noting that developments of this contractual kind have not occurred in other caring professions. In medicine, for example, the patient is almost entirely dependent on the doctor because of the nature of medical knowledge and skills. Indeed so dependent are clients in relation to many of these services that there has been a development of 'professional' social work support for clients in their dealings with the staff of agencies ostensibly designed to help. These developments have been particularly marked in the area of income support where clients are often assisted in claiming their full entitlement and in making appeals to tribunals if necessary. Similarly, people affected by planning proposals are sometimes assisted to present their views. The adversarial model of the legal system has been applied in these areas to some degree. Social workers often find themselves working for clients against other agencies in this way, though it is not clear that the client enjoys a different relationship with the social worker as a result. Once again the client must depend on the goodwill of workers and the controls exercised by their professional association. The client himself has no more power than he had in his direct social work relationships.

Interestingly we have not yet seen intervention of this sort on behalf of clients having problems with the personal social services. The caring orientation of such departments and their staff is assumed, or, where they exercise statutory powers that may be problematic (taking children or the mentally ill into care), recourse may be had to the courts to challenge their judgement. Perhaps we should come to accept that social workers, as they become members of a profession, are no different from other professionals in relation to their clientele. We may decide to rely on their ethical probity as an adequate safeguard of the client's interests, but that is certainly not what client participation means.

Group Work

Turning from case-work to the other areas of professional social work practice, the issues become very different. By its nature, group work tends not to involve the group and the social worker in any demands on people or agencies outside. The group itself, including the worker in many cases, practises a form of mutual therapy which necessarily involves member participation as the method is not otherwise possible. This participatory character is reinforced by other aspects of most group work. It is not necessary for individuals to participate and the consequent voluntary membership of a group gives a strong spur to active participation in group action or discussion. It also means that the worker organising the group can set conditions for group membership sure that only those who accept them will volunteer to participate. A further advantage is that group work techniques are usually advocated and adopted in non-crisis situations which facilitates participation by group members. All of these features make the technique a highly participatory one, though of course it is limited to the immediate group situation and to a restricted range of group members.

Despite these advantages the technique is not widely practised in the personal social services. The initiation of groups usually occurs at the initiative of a social worker and as yet few of them are trained in this kind of work. In most field-work situations in any case it is not easy to bring groups of clients together at the same time, particularly in face of very heavy demands from people experiencing immediate crises. The result has been a tendency for the technique to be used most often in residential settings or in long-stay hospitals where group members are readily available. Such settings may also give rise to rather less voluntary participation as staff have many more potential sanctions over possible group members.

Community Work

A third area of professional practice is also relatively under-developed (though increasing), but here the reasons may be of much greater significance for a general discussion of participation. Unlike case-work and much more than in group work, the 'clients' in community work enjoy the benefits of collective strength, though their degree of integration and solidarity vary from place to place. This advantage is reinforced by the fact that many people in the community are not clients in any usual sense of that word. Indeed a key feature of the community work approach is to expose the social worker to people who may need changes in their situation, but who often do not need individual help in the same way as case-work and group-work clients. This does not solve the problem of participation though it probably tends to equalise the relationship between the worker and the public or clients.

Two main sources of tension can arise in community work. One relates to the degree of participation involved. In this case it is not simply a matter of whether or not people are allowed to participate. Participation is the essence of this method and a directive approach on the part of the community worker can be understood as simply bad practice. The first problem is whether people want to participate to the degree involved in many varieties of community work. The second problem relates to the purposes for which their participation might be used. Unlike group work, community participation is not simply therapeutic for the people involved, it can also have significant instrumental purposes. The result is that one key problem becomes who should decide what community participation is for, and how conflicts over purposes are to be resolved. There is little unanimity over this. Community activity can range from self-help in building a playground or cleaning the area, to direct political action of various kinds to get the local authority to do those things

and many others. Moreover, such actions are not simply designed
to meet their obvious ends of more facilities or a cleaner environment. They may be seen as incidental to the development of community awareness and integration. Often this will be the community worker's main goal while the residents may simply want the
more obvious outcomes. The scope for conflict is obvious.

If this is a dilemma as between the community worker and the
community, it can also be a problem for the social services department, or any other agency, which employs community workers.
This can be overcome where communities employ their own workers, but our concern is with the more complicated three-cornered
relationship. As we noted in Chapter 3 the motives of those encouraging community work have been varied, and have changed
over time in the light of their experience. Thus the declining Home
Office interest in the national Community Development Project reflects an unwillingness on the part of government to support activity in local communities when it becomes radically critical of present social and political arrangements (CDP 1974). Similar responses can be seen in various localities where initiatives have been
stifled when they have taken unacceptable directions, unacceptable
that is to those in government (Pullen 1978). This is perfectly
understandable in the context of highly conflicting politics where
the generation of community action in traditionally deprived areas
has important implications. In relation to local government, unless
the community adopts a purely self-help perspective, action almost
certainly involves a threat to local councillors, and often to the influence of officials. It also involves a threat to other communities
locally, whether organised or not. Successful action by one community almost of necessity reduces the volume of service to others,
especially in a period of economic crisis. Politics is about the distribution of scarce public resources; community action is one
method of influencing that distribution.

Despite these fairly obvious tensions, social service departments
have continued to develop community work and, equally importantly, many staff have wanted to pursue a community work
approach. In the former case, given the pressures on departments,
staff can sometimes be placed in the difficult position of being expected to inhibit the actions of the community in which they work
in the interests of the local authority. They find themselves caught
between department and community, unable to serve both. Staff
with personal leanings towards community work find this potential
conflict extremely difficult, and frequently see their identification

with the community as of greatest importance. Not that this problem is inevitable or normal. Much community work is uncontentious and desirable and agreed between community and department. But in terms of participation the important problems arise when the local residents adopt a policy or approach which clashes with the department. Participation is encouraged as long as it remains within accepted and agreed guidelines.

This has led to debate about the role of the worker and the degree of direction which he should adopt in his relationships with local people. Community work, like case-work, can easily lead to professional dominance even though it is more difficult either to justify or to sustain. One solution would be to de-professionalise this area of work which would mean its almost complete removal from social service departments. One route which has been tried is the creation of separate community development departments, though they are equally prone to professionalism, and do not necessarily avoid the departmental problems. More detachment would be obtained by community workers operating from within the local community, though problems will remain both for the worker and for the supervising group. If community workers are employed and funded outside the local authority framework then they will not feel the tension of divided commitment nearly as much. They will lose some of the advantage of inside contact, but their relationship with the community will be much clearer and more amenable to community determination where that takes radical political forms. How such employment is funded, and how the ultimate impact of government (as for example through the Urban Programme or through Partnership) is avoided is a much wider question. Ultimately there will be political constraints imposed by conventional political institutions if they feel threatened. Separate employment will simply distance the worker from that effect: the ultimate clash will not be avoided.

OTHER SOCIAL SERVICES

We have dwelt at some length on those areas of social service provision which raise issues about participation. Other areas of social service work offer fewer opportunities in that direction. Many of them are routine in character: the provision of home help, for example, or of aids and appliances to the handicapped and of telephones to the housebound. In each of these cases there are reasonably clear bureaucratic rules about the allocation of the service and

Public participation in local services

little that the client can do within the context of those rules. It may
be that the rules are not appropriate and this could become an issue
for public debate and participation, but such a discussion would
embrace wider questions than our immediate concerns. The one
exception is in the area of residential care where there are obvious
issues about resident participation in children's homes or old people's homes. In the former case it may be that the age structure
militates against participation, or that the family unit style of home
is felt to overcome the problem. If residential care takes the family
form then children will participate with surrogate parents in the
same way as they do with real parents. This will vary with the
individuals concerned, but the context for participation is itself relatively straightforward.

The case of old people's homes is different. Ever since Peter
Townsend's *Last Refuge* (Townsend 1962) was written there has
been debate about the style and character of such accommodation.
From a staff perspective the ease of running a home may be facili-
tated by non-participation by the residents. Such an approach can
be justified in terms of their age and possible incompetence – the
latter being a common argument against participation in all fields.
From the point of view of the residents, participation may be crucial to their life-style and even to their life expectations. The
closed, or semi-open, institutional setting gives great power to the
staff, and again the prospects for participation look relatively bleak.
This is changing with the advent of smaller homes, better trained
staff and so on, but there is still a long way to go.

In this brief discussion of client participation the outstanding
impression must be of variety. Different kinds of social work have
quite different implications for participation and within each
approach there are further differences. Staff attitudes vary widely
about the merits of client participation, though the existence of a
community work option allows those staff who favour participation
to engage in that kind of work. At the same time departmental
needs must be considered and the constraints of political necessity
and resource limitation seem likely either to limit participation, or
to channel it in the direction of self-help. The tensions which these
broad considerations produce in many social service departments
are readily apparent. The advent of a fully qualified social work
staff and an increasingly aware and articulate clientele will not
make the situation any easier. One solution may be a clearer division of labour between the statutory sector and the voluntary sec-

tor. Each will perform its own best functions with the voluntary sector engaging the participant dimension more fully.

PARTICIPATION IN PROVISION

The history of the statutory provision of social services has been one of steady takeover from a wide range of charitable and voluntary bodies who have initially met various social needs. The pattern continues with the voluntary sector continuing to innovate in relation to needs such as provision for the single homeless, the care of alcoholics, or aspects of birth control advice. Once such services are clarified and legitimised by voluntary action, the State tends to become a direct service provider. But it never monopolises social care; nor indeed do the large number of voluntary social welfare organisations. Many others also provide social care. Families care for their dependants, both young and old. Neighbours give support to those living around them, often in material ways, but also by providing social support of various kinds. This pluralism of provision is another unusual feature of the personal social services.

The key questions about this aspect of social services include how much voluntary action there should be, and how it should relate to its statutory counterpart. Unlike the social worker's relationship with clients, in this case the two parties enjoy much more equal capacity. The voluntary bodies and volunteers can withdraw their services, leaving the local authorities to deal with the consequences. By the same token they can command some influence with local authorities by invoking that sanction of service removal, but also by using their knowledge of social need acquired through their direct service work. Of course the local authorities have their own weapons in any confrontation. Their obligations are quite well defined and they do not necessarily have to take over where volunteers withdraw. At the same time, for various reasons, local authorities often support voluntary action with cash or other resources and this can give them considerable influence over the voluntary sector.

The specialised role of voluntary organisations affects their attitudes towards participation. In the main in relation to personal social services, they are concerned with providing services. Far from wanting to promote or participate in wider public action, many organisations would be offended if their place was usurped by government. They would claim to provide a choice to clients, and often to provide a better service than their statutory counterparts. The accuracy of such claims is difficult to assess. If they are correct then we should perhaps not only maintain the voluntary movement, but seek to stimulate it more widely. Wherever voluntary bodies rely on public funding, however, it is invariably a case of either more voluntary and less statutory provision, or vice versa. Both cannot be maintained during periods of stringency: client choice is a luxury which tends to clash with the principles of good economy and the state principle of provision of services free at the point of consumption. Choice ultimately depends on surplus provision if it is to be real for many people.

If the claim to provide a better service is true, then we should be seeking to replace statutory services with those of volunteers. This is being done at the present time, and has been an element in government policy for some time, but not always to secure quality. It arises in part out of the search for economy and the relative cheapness of the volunteer, or voluntary body. If the cheaper alternative is not as good then we must acknowledge that the service is being diluted. In such circumstances should we be developing the voluntary element? From a client perspective probably not, but from a taxpayer perspective almost certainly yes. In such a context the willing flow of volunteers creates a high participant image, but may be detrimental to the quality of service, although it must always be remembered that voluntary social work can itself be a form of therapy for those who undertake it. If the provision rather than the service itself is seen as the social work input then obviously different criteria of success may be applied. It may be, however, that the selection of volunteers and voluntary agencies needs to be tightened up to protect clients from inferior service. Or that the degree of statutory supervision needs to be extended so as to secure more effective voluntary action. Either of these moves, and both are tending to happen, reduces the element of voluntarism involved and may undermine the participatory spirit which makes voluntary action so valuable.

These arguments do not apply to voluntary organisations which exist to press for better statutory services, or to operate as watchdogs on existing statutory provision. These are much rarer, and approximate closely to other pressure groups or to the sorts of community group discussed earlier. Their basis is normally related to some part of the social services clientele, but their aims are overtly political and often radical, at least in relation to incumbent councillors and officers. These organisations do not have the close relationship with the local authority enjoyed by the providers, though some organisations try to combine both tasks. Invariably it seems that an attempt to combine the tasks reverts to acting basically as a provider, and perhaps using the close contact which results to seek marginal changes within the local authority. Straight pressure for change or improvement depends for its success on the client group involved, the general climate affecting change, the resources and skill of the group, and the attitudes and political security of the particular local council. Given the obvious difficulties it is not surprising that one can find few examples of successful pressure. Demonstrating by providing is much more likely to be successful than political pressure by non-providers. Only in rare circumstances of politically marginal control will there be real opportunities for influence, and even in these circumstances the personal social services are not usually highly conspicuous in local politics.

In short there is considerable participation but of a very particular kind. Much of the involvement of voluntary groups with the local authority is organised so as to maintain this situation and minimise the likelihood of alternative voluntary action. When the local authority is concerned at the possible participatory pressures from voluntary organisations, it has several strategies open to limit their effect. As we have said, voluntary dependence of local government finance presents one obvious means. The threat of withdrawal of grant, and the occasional carrying out of such a threat, can have a powerful effect. Another way is to co-opt representative volunteers on to social service committees and sub-committees, or even to create special liaison arrangements to facilitate voluntary input. In the former cases the voluntary sector gets to participate in 'decision-making' directly, though the dominant ethos of party politics and majority rule in local government means that their influence is heavily constrained. Voluntary representatives are also constrained in other ways on such committees. They have little knowledge, apart from the experience gained in their own organisations, and cannot therefore inject much in the way of wider skilled information or counsel. This puts them at a disadvantage by comparison with senior local government officers. In relation to councillors, the volunteer has limited legitimacy, representing only his own organisation or personal views. Confronted by a combination of officer and councillor, the co-optee must be weak. And if this is not enough constraint, co-optees suffer from being present in service committees but absent when the vital resource allocations are made in party groups or policy committees.

Many voluntary organisations would acknowledge these limitations, but would argue that co-opted membership gives them access to 'inside dope' which is invaluable to external campaigning and to understanding the purposes of the local authority. This is true, though the price of knowing is often an embargo on using the information. At worst it cannot be used and at best it has to be used surreptitiously. In terms of a providing voluntary organisation this may not matter and the development of a clear symbiosis between local authority and voluntary organisation may be strengthened. For organisations with other interests, co-optation clearly inhibits their activities.

CONCLUSIONS

It is clear from this chapter that participation in the personal social services is equivocal. At the level of the individual client there is a sharp imbalance between client and worker. Commitment to giving the client more say in that relationship is common as we have seen in the Seebohm Report and in the ethical code adopted by social workers. Yet at the same time there are tendencies in the social services in quite the opposite direction. Respect for the client's rights has to compete with increased professionalism among social workers and more complex notions about client problems and how they might be treated. It is hard to be optimistic about client participation in such circumstances. The best that seems likely is a developing consumerism or some slight increase in the rate of individual success by clients. There are no signs of any wider development at the individual level and no momentum for a change in the climate of client–worker relationships. Indeed at this individual level greater client success may militate against wider change. Those who succeed enjoy differential advantage as long as the system remains unchanged and this can reduce their interest in more general improvement.

Community work and the developing activity of voluntary organisations might offer greater potential for wider impact through participation. In theory they are concerned with wider issues than those affecting individual clients, and each involves a collective group drawn from either a geographical area or from a client group. Yet both face problems in trying to generate effective participation. Their potential may be great, but the means to achieve it are often not available. Much power continues to remain with the local authority social services department. The community worker is often employed by the department and his ambivalence when faced with conflict of interest is obvious. In the case of voluntary organisations there is often a shared interest with the local authority which goes well beyond their concern for the clientele. Financial relationships and a joint wish to carry on providing services can mute any voluntary statements about the statutory services. Where those mutual interests are less developed there is a tendency for the local authority to see the voluntary group in much more negative terms. The absence of 'rights' of access for such outside groups, and the presence of more formal and more legitimate political processes, weaken their case considerably.

Dependency is perhaps the key to this area of service. Clients are obviously dependent, for service and support. The threat of losing either may be enough to limit their participation if it is critical of the department. People in local communities are also dependent: for information, for training, for skills and for other resources. They often have to seek assistance from the very departments they wish to attack. Voluntary organisations too are dependent. Their close ties with government make them dependent for cash, and sometimes for cases to sustain their programme of assistance. Participation is centrally about changing this dependency: it is the Catch-22 of such work that you need to be independent before you can participate.

Education is the largest of the services provided for the public by local authorities. Only housing can match the demands education makes upon local public expenditure, and housing, of course, is largely a matter of capital expenditure financed by long-term borrowing. Education accounts for about half the current expenditure of local authorities; no other service reaches much more than 10 per cent. Education is also a major employer. Over 600,000 teachers work for local authorities and they are supported by a similar number of employees in administrative, technical and manual occupations – everyone from the Chief Education Officer to the dinner lady and the caretaker. The shadow of education is, therefore, continually present in discussions of local government finance and the determination of priorities between local government services. For this reason we might expect considerable debate about both the resources devoted to education and the division of these resources among the various branches of the service. Public participation in these debates might be expected to be lively and consistent. Such expectations have not usually been fulfilled. Until recently there has been a general assumption that money spent on education, almost *any* amount of money, was a 'good thing'. Within such a climate the only participation that seemed appropriate was to press for greater expenditure: to which pressure educationalists, whether administrators or teachers, were only too eager to respond.

In the past few years as the birth-rate has fallen, and the squeeze on public expenditure has become sharper, education has had to defend itself; but, again, public involvement in these broad questions of resource allocation has not been very great. Local education authorities have in some parts of the country decided to end school transport or meals, to restrict or end nursery provision, to increase adult education fees to unprecedented heights, or even to abolish the adult education service altogether. These decisions, where they have been made, have aroused protests, but the public has only been able to participate through the usual methods of council elections or public pressure. At first sight this seems surprising as education and participation are frequently linked together in general discussion, but a distinction must be made between these broader resource issues and those matters of administration and practice where public involvement is frequently encouraged. A further distinction needs to be made between participation in policy and administration and participation as an integral part of the educational process.

Public interest in educational policy is a natural reflection of parental concern to influence a process which may affect their children's religious, social and political attitudes, as well as their opportunities in later life. This 'hidden curriculum' through which teachers and schools convey the attitudes of one generation to the next is frequently of more significance to parents than the subject matter being taught. Hence the controversies over the introduction of comprehensive education were conducted around the style of school that would result and, covertly, the social mix of the pupils who would attend, rather than around the subjects that might be taught in the sixth form. Parents often wish to maintain the trappings of the great nineteenth-century schools: the uniforms and formal discipline, even corporal punishment; but above all they want their children to leave school having been taught in their own image.

Within the past twenty years changes have been introduced into the local authority education service that have reawakened the controversies that are never far from the surface when discussing education. The changes have been concerned both with the institutional structure of the schools and their management, and with the methods adopted in the teaching. The Labour Government's introduction of comprehensive schools to replace the tripartite structure that had existed since the 1944 Education Act was opposed by most Conservative councils – and by many middle class parents – though not by some liberal-minded parents' organisations. The changes in the teaching method, on the other hand, have been spearheaded by the Schools Council which has reflected the growing interest among teachers in *how* rather than *what* children learn. During this period there has been an increasing emphasis on raising the level of initial and post-experience training for teachers which is steadily becoming a graduate profession. The Schools Council has represented this growing professional self-confidence.

Those parents who wish to participate in discussions over these developments have found themselves confronted, therefore, by two sets of constraints. First, the major institutional changes, such as those relating to comprehensive education or the trend towards larger schools, were being decided at national level on party political lines. Second, decisions about the content and methods of education were being taken by teachers who claimed the unchallengeable authority of full professionalism.

A discussion of participation in educational matters is further complicated by the nature of the service. Education is an integral part of the development of each individual person and depends for success on the interaction between teacher and pupil. Nor is the participation of the pupil alone sufficient: in the case of children, parental support is increasingly recognised as a key factor in educational development. If there is a conflict between the values of home and school then the education of the child will suffer. Progressive educationalists have, therefore, stressed the need for parental involvement in support of a school's objectives. At the same time, some parents have sought to influence the content of those objectives in the face of strong opposition from those teachers who adopt a narrow interpretation of professionalism.

When we turn from schools to other aspects of the educational service, a further dimension in the relationship between participation and education becomes apparent. A participatory society requires an educational service that will support participants, both actual and potential, in the development of the skills necessary for effective intervention. The approach of the educationalist may encourage people either into an acceptance of existing arrangements, or to challenge the policies with which they are presented. In either case, the relationship between education and social attitudes is made plain without the obscuring effect of the professed teaching of particular subjects in particular ways for the subject's own sake. Participation, in education, therefore, is not simply a matter of taking part in the determination of policy, it enters into the discussions of methods, and may even become one of the objectives of the process itself. These three aspects are obviously interrelated, but we shall find it convenient to discuss some of the principal developments from each in turn and we shall start with the institutional arrangements.

In the controversies surrounding the introduction of a publicly provided service in 1870, religious considerations predominated: education was already being provided both by church organisations and by private foundations and they viewed the incursion of the State with considerable suspicion. The reasons for state intervention are of interest. First, the existing system was providing neither a workforce capable of competing in technical knowledge with overseas manufacturers, nor the standard of literacy required in the administrative and professional occupations that were growing in number. Second, there was an interest in the newly enfranchised town artisans accepting their position within the existing social framework. In a famous speech in the House of Commons in 1867, Robert Lowe said: 'It will be absolutely necessary that you should prevail on our future masters to learn their letters' (Armytage 1965: 139). This concern both with the relationship between the educational system and the needs of industry, and with the effect of education upon the structure of society has been reflected in more recent debates. The occasional pleas to keep politics out of education are no more than a misunderstanding both of politics and of education: their authors certainly cannot point to any historical precedents.

The great debates which surrounded the introduction of state education have bequeathed us an administrative system in which an attempt is made to balance the various interests concerned. Education is frequently described as a national service, locally administered; and there are also opportunities both for the involvement of voluntary bodies in the provision of their own schools, and for people who are not elected members of the local education authority to be involved in the management of the service.

The basis of the present system is the 1944 Education Act. Under section 1 the Minister (now the Secretary of State for Education) has a duty:

... to promote the education of the people of England and Wales and the progressive development of institutions devoted to that purpose, and to secure the effective execution by local authorities, under his control and direction, of the national policy for providing a varied and comprehensive educational service in every area.

The term comprehensive did not have the special meaning it came to possess from the 1950s, but section 1 clearly indicates the potential for central direction existing within the 1944 Act. The local education authorities on the other hand, have a duty under the Act (Education Act 1944: section 7), '... so far as their powers extend, to contribute towards the spiritual, moral, mental and physical development of the community by securing that efficient education throughout those stages shall be available to meet the needs of the population of their area'. There are detailed provisions concerning the manner in which these requirements shall be judged and, of course, the Secretary of State has the benefit of the advice of Her Majesty's Inspectors of Schools when considering particular cases.

Despite the strong words of the 1944 Act, the local education authorities are not mere puppets of central government. The Act specifies the context within which the general powers of the Secretary of State may be exercised and local education authorities are allocated some areas of discretion or even power to determine local policy. The wide divergence of practice throughout the country should dispel any thought of a uniform education service imposed by Westminster and Whitehall. Professor David Regan (1977: 35) considers:

. . . the DES has much more power than the old, pre-war Board of Education, and more than most government departments today over their respective services. The DES is, however, characterised more by promotionalism, deep involvement in the service, than by a hierarchical dictatorial determination to enforce its will. . . . In any case there are substantial areas of education where no DES control exists, and it is no simple matter for the DES to increase its powers statutorily.

Simple matter or no, the government has been increasingly willing to try. The resultant political furore, particularly over the introduction of comprehensive education, has involved both local authorities and parents although Parliament has ultimately determined the matter, and then reversed its decision, without any fine regard for local public opinion.

Parents of every child of compulsory school age are also given duties in the 1944 Act (Section 36). They must, '. . . cause him to receive efficient full-time education suitable to his age, ability and aptitude, either by regular attendance at school or otherwise'. The opportunity of educating a child at home is accepted by a few parents, but they must be able to satisfy the local education authority, or ultimately the courts, of their ability to fulfil their statutory obligations. Of more significance is the possibility of organising a school outside the state system.

The integration of private and public provision is more fully developed in education than in other local services, although parallels may be found in co-operative housing schemes supported by the Housing Corporation. The existence of an influential private section of education before the introduction of a compulsory obligation on parents to cause their children to be educated led to various measures of support being given to schools outside the public sector. In these cases parents, either as individuals, or more usually through religious or charitable organisations, were given statutory rights to participate in the provision of a public service. The 'voluntary schools', as they are called, may be either 'controlled' or 'aided' depending upon the amount of financial assistance received from the local authority. Local authorities accept full financial responsibility for controlled schools, but in return appoint two-thirds of the governors or managers and all the teachers. The original foundation retains ownership, and the parents the right to request that their children receive religious instruction in accordance with the school's original denomination, but control is in effect little different from that of local authority schools. The 'aided' schools, which include the Roman Catholic schools, have more freedom. The local authority only appoints one-third of the governors or managers and the foundation appoints both the headteacher and the assistant teachers. The foundation retains complete control of the religious syllabus in both primary and secondary aided schools, but of the secular syllabus in secondary schools only. The cost of aided schools is shared between the local authority and the foundation. The local authority pays for the upkeep of the interior of the building and for all educational costs including teachers' salaries. The foundation is responsible for the exterior of the building and for any improvements, although it receives grants of up to 80 per cent direct from central government in respect of these responsibilities.

The conjunction between private initiative and public funding reaches its nadir in the independent schools. As their name implies they are not subject to local authority control, but neither do they receive any direct financial assistance. Some indirect support is available from local authorities through the nomination of pupils for whom the fees are paid from public funds. Whereas most of the 'voluntary' schools are religious foundations, the 'independent' schools vary widely from the great public schools to small local 'prep' schools and schools associated with particular educational philosophies. Most of them are controlled by a charitable trust and although they are subject to government inspection the criteria for acceptance are wide enough to allow a range of practice from the formality of some grammar schools to the liberal atmosphere of A.S. Neill's Summerhill or the more recent 'free school movement'.

Public participation in local services

Participation in the provision of the service can fade imperceptibly into a simple element of choice as the influence of individual consumers is overshadowed by corporate charities or a church. In such cases the description 'public participation' is no more appropriate than it would be in any other area of consumer choice. We do not customarily consider that we are participating in decisions affecting public transport policy, for example, if we choose to use a private car. As we have indicated, the position in the education service is complicated both by the compulsory nature of the service – nobody is legally compelled to use transport – and by the complex relationships between public and private provision. In several areas of the country the opportunity to provide schooling outside the local authority system, yet with some support from public funds, has given groups of parents a basis from which to challenge educational policy. The parents concerned are mostly those with either strong religious convictions or the ability to pay substantial school fees, but their participation has been important, particularly during disputes over the introduction of comprehensive education. During these disputes 'aided' schools have often been given the option of becoming part of the new system or of becoming completely independent: and independent schools have lost the income from the fees of local authority nominated pupils as these became an anachronism in a comprehensive system. Despite these pressures, the powers of delay available to the schools and parents concerned have sometimes been sufficient for them to await a council or government more sympathetic to their views following an election.

The element of parental choice has become entangled in the public mind, therefore, with developments more specifically relating to public participation. The important point for many parents has been how they could gain control over the type of education their children would receive – whether within the state system, or by opting for one of the other possibilities. Representation on managing bodies or public funding for private schools has been seen by some parents (though not by the more philosophically minded members of the Confederation for State Education) as alternative means to the same objectives. The parents who adopt such attitudes have been predominantly middle class, and the extension of parental choice has consequently become an important plank in the educational policy of the Conservative party. In opposition it considered the possibility of introducing 'educational vouchers' which parents could 'spend' at either a private or a local authority school, but in government the party did not find this a practicable possibility. It introduced instead a scheme whereby the government reimburses the fees chargeable in respect of pupils selected for assisted places at certain independent schools. The Education (No. 2) Act 1980, also returned some discretion to local authorities which had been removed by the previous Labour administration, and introduced formal procedures for parents wishing to choose the local authority school their children would attend. Local authorities are no longer compelled to introduce comprehensive education, but they must make arrangements for enabling parents to express a preference as to the school their child should attend and to give reasons for their preference. The local authority must make information available to parents on their admission arrangements and provide for appeals against their decisions. The Act also contains provisions for parental representation on managing bodies, but we shall refer to these later in the chapter.

The support given to these aspects of Conservative policy by many parents emphasises a reluctance to grant control over education to a representative body without allowing for some parental choice and a measure of public participation in broad policy decisions. Such participation is already allowed for both through co-option to education committees of local authorities and by the establishment of boards of governors for schools. These provisions are more extensive than those existing for other local services where co-option is rare and management bodies which include non-council members are seldom given even the minimal executive functions enjoyed by school governors.

The 1944 Education Act, following earlier legislation, enjoins each education committee to 'include persons of experience in education and persons acquainted with the educational conditions prevailing in the area for which the committee acts' (Schedule One). In a few cases local authorities consider that these requirements can be met from within their own elected membership, but usually a number of non-council members are co-opted to the education committee. Many councils take advantage of this provision to recruit party supporters from trades councils and chambers of commerce, together with representatives of churches and teachers' unions. Sometimes representatives of other educational institutions such as a local university or the Workers' Educational Association are appointed, and occasionally a few places are found for parents' organisations. The prevalent use of the powers of co-option to appoint active party members to join their elected colleagues on the education committee means that the committee seldom changes its representative character. The elected members are very much in control, as indeed the Act intends, and the most unusual aspect of the education committee is frequently the appearance of teachers. As employees of the local authority they are ineligible for election to the council, but since 1902 they may be co-opted to the education committee as full members. The teachers' trade unions naturally press local authorities to exercise this power which allows teachers to be represented during important policy discussions in committee. Pressure groups representing parents are not co-opted as frequently as teachers and they must rely usually on the indirect representation provided by the councillors.

The growing power of the teaching profession in the determination of educational policy is manifest in other, and arguably more important, ways than in their more frequent appearance on education committees. Many teachers were prominent in support of the introduction of comprehensive education and the National Union of Teachers gave the policy official support from 1966. More significant for their growing claims to full professionalism has been the role of teachers in the Schools Council for the Curriculum Examinations. This government funded body contains forty-five teacher members among the eighty members of the governing council. The Schools Council has developed many new approaches for teaching and has exerted steady pressure for the classroom teacher to have greater control over the nature and content of examinations. By 1980 the General Secretary of the National Association of Head Teachers could speak of a 'traditional partnership within the education service between Government, local authorities and teachers' (*The Times* 27 May 1980).

Parents were conspicuously absent from this view of 'the traditional partnership' but in fact there has been a growing pressure both for a closer involvement of parents in the management of schools and for a recognition of the crucial part they play in the education of their children. This pressure has come from both progressive educationalists and parental organisations; but the teachers' organisations have been worried at a perceived threat to their professional status, and parental involvement is still actively discouraged in many schools. English schools have traditionally been free from outside pressures: the headteacher is dominant in determining the ethos of the school; and the class teacher has considerable independence in the methods employed in the classroom.

These arrangements are challenged by a participatory approach from several directions. First, the teachers themselves are gaining more influence in their own schools as more headteachers adopt consensual rather than autocratic styles of leadership. Second, the public (and their elected representatives), parents, and in some cases older pupils, are expecting to discuss matters of educational policy and classroom practice more frequently than in the past. The teachers, therefore, feel that their professional status in the schools, which is growing as they struggle free from autocratic headteachers, is being immediately threatened by the emergence of 'parent power'. These fears, especially among younger and progressive teachers, are compounded when parents seek to maintain traditional approaches to uniforms and discipline, and question the new teaching methods and forms of assessment and examination.

The implied conflict of approach which many teachers fear between their professional status and parental participation was undoubtedly accentuated by the 'Black Paper' attacks on many of the innovations in education, but these attacks certainly did not represent the views of all parents. The parents' major national pressure groups have adopted a generally progressive stance. The Confederation for the Advancement of State Education (CASE) was formed in 1960 and now has many local branches. It also has close links with the Home and Schools Council and with the National Association of Governors and Managers. The membership has been drawn disproportionately from the liberal, professional middle class and their policy from 1965 has favoured comprehensive education. CASE also opposes any extension of denominational education and is in favour of co-educational schools, but for our present purposes the most important aspect of its policy is concerned with pressing for greater parental involvement. In a statement of objectives in 1974, CASE stated: 'There should be detailed information available about every school, choice of schools, parent–teachers' associations where the majority of parents want one, and parents and teachers represented on school governors' (Kogan 1974: 127).

The 1944 Education Act placed a responsibility on local education authorities to provide 'for the constitution of the body of managers or governors' for every county, that is, local authority school (section 17). The managers served for primary schools and the governors for secondary schools. The Education (No. 2) Act 1980 removed the distinction and governors are now appointed for both primary and secondary schools. The Department of Education and Science must approve local authorities' proposals for governors, but in practice over the years a wide range of schemes has been approved. In some cases a sub-committee of the education committee has assumed the functions of the managing or governing board for *all* the primary or secondary schools in the area. In other cases schools have been grouped with one board covering several schools. Membership of the boards has often been confined to education committee members or their nominees and has sometimes been regarded as an extension of political patronage for the majority party. Parents of children in a particular school have sometimes been excluded from membership in an extreme extension of the 'conflict of interest' principle that prevents council tenants, for example, voting on housing issues if they are members of a local authority.

During the 1970s attitudes changed considerably. The membership of school boards of managers or governors in many areas began to include elected representatives of both parents and teachers, and the number of schools with individual managing or governing bodies began to increase. The growing interest in school managers and governors resulted in the appointment of a departmental committee under the chairmanship of Councillor Tom Taylor with the following terms of reference:

To review the arrangements for the management and government of maintained primary and secondary schools in England and Wales, including the composition and functions of bodies of managers and governors, and their relationships with local education authorities, with head teachers and staffs of schools, with parents of pupils and with the local community at large; and to make recommendations.

The Taylor Committee Report in 1977 carried the significant title, *A New Partnership for Our Schools* and in their preface the authors outlined six principles which had guided their thinking. These included a concern 'for promoting and protecting good relationships both within the school and between the school and its parents and the wider community' (Taylor Committee 1977: xii). They believed that the governing body should have delegated responsibility for running the school and that no one interest should be dominant among the governors. The recommendations followed from these principles. A separate governing body should be set up for each primary and secondary school which should consist of equal numbers of local education authority representatives, school staff, elected parents and representatives of the local community. The establishment of more open boards of governors was seen to imply a more open system of decision-making throughout the

structure. There were, therefore, recommendations about the need
for the headteacher to consult the teaching staff on day-to-day matters, and for parents to have the right to set up their own organisations with appropriate facilities for their activities within the
school. The Committee also recommended that provision should be
made for initial and inservice training for governors.

The functions of these new governing bodies would be concerned with every aspect of the school: the determining of its aims;
consideration of the means by which these should be pursued; and
reviewing the progress being made. The local education authority,
acting within the framework of legislation, would obviously retain
control of the overall structure of the education service within an
area, and of the allocation of financial and other resources; but
within these constraints there would be no separation of responsibility between professional staff and lay governors. In two key paragraphs the Committee wrote of the 'modern developments in curriculum theory and practice' which had 'worried many people not
involved in school education' (para. 6.18), and rejected as artificial
any attempt to distinguish between 'an element of essentially in-
structional responsibility to be assigned to the school's head and his
colleagues, and other elements of a more administrative, social or
political kind in which other people – be they governors or the local
education authorities – might play an important part' (para. 6.19).
The teachers through their organisations described the Taylor Report as 'a busybodies charter', but both the Labour and Conservative parties gave support to its general approach without commit-
ting themselves to implement the recommendations in full. The
Education (No. 2) Act 1980 provides for at least two elected parents
to be appointed to every board of governors, and for at least one
(two if the school has more than 300 pupils) elected teacher in
addition to the headteacher. The grouping of schools for governing
purposes is still permissible under the Act, but in most cases it now
needs the approval of the Secretary of State and the general impression is that separate boards for each school will be encouraged.
The implementation of these provisions will proceed as resources
become available.

The implementation of these provisions will mean a large increase in the number of places available on school boards. In
Sheffield, for example, where similar boards to those the Taylor
Committee proposed were introduced in 1970, there are about
5,000 school managers or governors in a city with half-a-million
population. Such numbers pose problems both of recruitment and

of administration. At least three board meetings a year need to be arranged, clerked and minuted for each of several hundred schools. In Sheffield a small section of the Education Office is completely occupied with this work and about 150 officers share the clerking duties. One of the advantages claimed for the system is indeed the opportunity it gives to officials from the education office to learn about the problems schools are facing. With such large numbers involved there are occasional difficulties in recruitment; in particular parents do not turn up in large numbers to election meetings. However, over the years since Sheffield introduced the broader membership, the places have been filled, and there have been frequent contests for the elected seats. The school boards in Sheffield have fulfilled neither the high hopes of the Taylor Committee, nor the worst fears of the headteachers and other teachers' organisations. They have done a quiet rather than spectacular job in extending the community links of individual schools through an increase in the number of parent–school associations. They have seldom challenged the authority of the headteacher, and only rarely discussed the curriculum with any real sense of purpose. There has been a disappointing tendency to discuss the fabric of the buildings, or the state of the plumbing, at inordinate length, and to spend time on self-congratulatory chat about the achievements of the netball team. In many cases the boards are deliberately led in this direction by the headteachers. The local authority, on the other hand, has sought to extend the range of school board discussions by including on the agenda discussion papers on current educational topics ranging from the teaching of French in junior schools to the effect on secondary schools of falling school rolls. The opinions expressed have been a useful indication of school opinion which the clerks could carry back to the education office. The discussions have also been a channel through which the education office could stimulate thought in the schools on current topics. The Bullock Report on the teaching of English, to which we shall refer later in this chapter, received widespread attention in this way.

In a thoughtful analysis of the first few years of the reformed school boards in Sheffield, Dr William Bacon concluded that the educational establishment – the senior councillors and officials of the Education Committee – were the main beneficiaries of the new system (Bacon 1978). The boards discuss topics which need to be publicised, and defuse contentious issues by moving the locus of discontent from the Education Committee to the school managers or governors. The boards also form a useful support force for the Education Department as it becomes immersed in the more competitive struggle for resources implied in the centralised corporate structure of a changing local authority. Several thousand local people regularly discuss the needs of *their* school and usually press for improvements of one kind or another. Power over the resources obtained remains firmly in the hands of the Education Committee; no significant power has, in Dr Bacon's view, been devolved either to parents or to board members.

There is no doubting the force of Dr Bacon's arguments if participation is judged by the reallocation of formal power. The creation of more open systems of public administration does not of itself determine the outcome of policy discussions. Experienced politicians and administrators may use these systems to manipulate a consent that would be withheld in a closed political environment. But such considerations do not deny the advantages of living in an open rather than a closed society. Thousands of people in Sheffield have learned a little more about the education service and have experienced the opportunity to express their views in a formal setting. Some decisions have been modified; many more have been defended in open debate; much more information has become available to many more people. These are not inconsiderable additions to a representative system of local government, even if they do not constitute a participatory society.

The provision of more open government or administration through co-option to education committees or through more representative school boards is not the only way in which the concept of participation enters educational debates. The process of education itself requires the active participation of the recipient of the services if it is to be successful. Just as one can lead a horse to the water without being able to make him drink, so a compulsory educational service does not necessarily result in an educated society. The pupil must actively engage in the learning process if the desired results are to be obtained. The introduction of teaching methods designed to facilitate this process has been among the contentious issues raised by the approach of the Schools' Council and progressive educationalists. A more questioning attitude has been encouraged among pupils that may affect their willingness to accept hierarchical structures of command in other contexts. In this sense participatory educational methods may be one factor in the creation of the demand for more open decision-taking that we are discussing throughout this book. There are other aspects of this approach, however, which are even more closely related to such developments as the introduction of broadly based boards of managers or governors; educational theories which stress the significance of parental and community support for the success a child achieves at school.

Several of the influential reports on aspects of the educational service which were written in the 1960s and 1970s emphasised the importance of links between home and school. The Plowden Report, for example, recommended the creation of educational priority areas where a community work approach would be used to stimulate parental involvement. The subsequent experimental projects and the report written by Professor Halsey and his colleagues formed an important part of the community work initiatives which are referred to in Chapter 3 above. The Plowden Report was not without its critics. Some sociologists believed that it underestimated the social principles which are responsible for the shaping of attitudes and the same critics pointed to the increasingly 'specialised teaching techniques which are difficult for the parent to learn' (R.S. Peters 1969: 69–70). Despite these criticisms, the Plowden Report has exercised a strong influence on educational thinking. The traditional separation of home and school, symbolised by the line drawn on the playground beyond which parents should not pass, is gradually being replaced by a more open attitude. The Taylor Committee saw the fostering of such developments as an important function of their new governing bodies, and the concept of the 'community school' is gaining ground both at primary and at secondary level.

The Plowden Report was concerned to encourage parental and community *support* for schools; parental participation was still subordinate to the professional judgements of the teachers and seldom impinged on their teaching role. The more recent Bullock Report (1975) on teaching the use of English recognised the important part played by parents in educating their own children. A child begins to acquire language skills before commencing school and will progress more surely if the parents and other adults with whom he or she comes into contact are aware of the importance of encouraging language development. The school needs to extend into the home to assist parents to understand their educational role; but equally parents are needed in the school to provide the increased adult contact which is believed to stimulate their children's facility for the use of language. Parents are being encouraged to participate in a partnership not in this instance concerned with the management of the service, but with its very purpose – the education of their children.

The developments sketched in the previous few paragraphs indicate the complexity of the relationship between education and public participation. Larger local authorities and schools, together with the integration of education into corporate management structures, make it advantageous for educational administrators to create decentralised school boards for consultative purposes. At the same time, developments in educational theory and practice stress the importance of parental participation in the educational process. Parents, and other members of the public, who press for greater opportunities to participate in the determination of policy for the service find themselves invited, therefore, into structures which serve purposes rather different from those they had expected – and where more experienced politicians and professionals determine the rules. In this respect, the lay participants in education may only reflect more clearly the ambiguities surrounding public participation that are present in all the initiatives of the past few years. The phrase 'public participation' went through a period of great popularity without suffering too great an exactitude in its meaning. We discuss these problems of definition elsewhere, but there is one other dimension of the relationship between public participation and education that is appropriate to this chapter.

There is a long and honourable tradition, stretching back to Socrates, of education for citizenship. Indeed, from one point of view, the whole purpose of education is to enable people to enter and control their physical and social environment. The growing interest in public participation in the provision of public services or in the discussion of public policy that we are considering brings forward a need for education in the procedures and policies involved. People who enter the public arena need help in developing the confidence and gaining the knowledge that will enable them to meet existing policy-makers on more equal terms. The Russell Report (1973) on adult education contained the following statement:

The way of democracy is to submit areas of controversy to debate, in the belief that right judgements are built upon knowledge, critical enquiry and rational discussion. Those who lack the knowledge, or the tools of enquiry and expression, and who thereby feel excluded from a say in the decisions that govern their lives, are effectively disenfranchised.

The meeting of these needs was considered by the Russell Report 'to be one of the prime needs of the future' (Russell Report

1973: 12). Some of the other reports concerned with public participation also mentioned the educational implications of their proposals. The report on industrial democracy recommended the spending of over £3 million in the first three years after the introduction
of worker directors (Bullock Report 1977). The report was not implemented, but public money is made available through the Workers' Educational Association and the Trades Union Congress Educational Service for the training of shop stewards, and employee
representatives appointed under the Health and Safety legislation.
The Taylor Committee on school management was less specific
about cost, but equally convinced that its proposals would 'create a
need for training in effective participation' (Taylor Report 1977).
Given the numbers of school governors implied by their proposals,
this training could prove a challenging commitment for adult
education agencies.

A recent survey by one of the present authors was conducted to
discover how far educational agencies were meeting the educational
needs arising from the growing interest in a more informed and
participatory democracy (Hampton 1980). The results of the survey
were interesting but scarcely impressive. Over two-thirds of the
agencies responding provided some 'educational activities to assist
people to participate in public affairs or to understand and discuss
public issues', but the extent of their provision was small. There
was no evidence of agencies having thought through policies concerning this aspect of their work. Often other local authority departments such as social services or planning were providing support for participants without recognising the educational nature of
their work. In some cases, community workers were specifically
rejecting assistance from education authorities which they suspected of imposing predetermined patterns on the participatory
activities of the people with whom they were working (Hampton
1979).

From the range of activities provided by educational agencies
several examples are especially relevant for our present purposes.
These are concerned with either stimulating public awareness of
public issues or preparing members of the public who wish to
undertake an active role in public life. Adult education agencies
organise conferences on topics as diffuse as women's rights and
nuclear energy. In a few cases quite elaborate co-operation with local authority planning departments has enabled courses to be provided to assist people wanting to contribute to the statutory processes for participation in planning. Groups have come together to

consider different aspects of the planning needs in an area, relating these to the preliminary work or draft proposals of the planning authority with the assistance of a planning officer. The discussions have been helped by the presence of an adult education tutor who has also advised the group on the formulation of its submissions to the local authority. This co-operation between some planning authorities and adult education has resulted in groups preparing responses to public participation exercises which were based on a much more systematic analysis of the issues involved.

For some public roles, the acceptance of training is a condition of appointment: magistrates and the 1,600 volunteers who make up the Children's Panels in Scotland come within this category. Opportunities also exist for many thousands of shop stewards and health and safety representatives to attend courses during their working time. For most other people the opportunities are limited, but experience suggests no lack of response when appropriate provision is provided. In Hamilton, for example, several hundred people have been assisted with the techniques necessary for the efficient performance of their duties as officers of voluntary organisations or community groups; and thousands of school managers and governors throughout the country have been helped by courses concerned with educational policy and administration.

Adult education for participation is not without its difficulties. Indeed, the political consequences of educational work intended to promote political understanding and involvement can scarcely be avoided. The Russell Committee considered: 'If adult education has not hitherto been outstandingly successful in meeting this need, it is partly because of a certain unwillingness to become entangled with controversy (Russell Report 1973: 12). People may often need help in understanding procedures or political processes to enable them to contest local authority policies. The adult education tutor who is employed by that same local authority needs to exercise some caution. The position may be even *more* sensitive if the tutor is involved with a group opposing the policy of another local authority as can happen when education and housing within an area are the responsibility of different local authorities. One local education officer gave the following advice in an effort to contain potential difficulties between adult education tutors and elected representatives: 'The tutor is expected to tell them which door to knock on, even what banner to carry, but *not* be at the head of the queue.' (From an interview with one of the authors.)

Over the past few years as we have indicated, plenty of parents have been knocking on many doors and the debates about education show no signs of declining. Nor are the controversies confined to the local level although they are often sharpest during confrontations between parents and local authorities over comprehensive organisation or the closure of a particular school. The 'great debate' on education initiated by Mr Callaghan as Prime Minister never really developed; but there is a constant concern to relate schools and the curriculum more closely to 'national needs'. In the discussions about educating children for the future needs of industry and for a changing society we are reminded once again of the original reasons for state intervention referred to at the beginning of this chapter; and of the essentially political nature of questions about educational policy. In their attempts to influence public opinion and the thinking of teachers and local authorities, successive governments have issued consultation papers and appointed various committees of inquiry. Their encouragement of public participation in these debates through parents' organisations and governing bodies indicates the special position education occupies among public services: the involvement of the State in the education of children remains a matter of sensitive concern. So strongly is this recognised that the legislation places a considerable responsibility upon the parents themselves who are expected to want a greater degree of involvement in education than they want in some other local services. Not only are parents expected to want this involvement, but it is thought to be necessary if children are to receive the full benefits of the education being provided. The education service then comes full circle as it helps parents and other members of the community prepare themselves for participation in education and other local services. Public participation cannot, therefore, be separated from education: the two concepts are integrally related.

This book has reviewed the experience of participation in relation to a number of public goods and services which are delivered on a local basis, and has examined participation in neighbourhood and community terms. Clearly the extent to which the public is involved in policy-making and service provision varies from service to service. It depends on the extent to which such services are provided on a client or a collective basis; how highly professionalised they are; and on the scale of involvement expected by both public and providers. We will examine the context of, and the constraints on, participation which are set by the different services more fully later. First we return to the concept of participation more generally.

In an earlier publication, we concluded by stressing the importance of participation in providing for the political education of the public in its broadest sense (Boaden *et al.* 1980). From the Greeks onwards this has been a recurrent and ultimate goal of all liberal democrats who believe that the politically educated citizen is well able to perform his democratic role in society: exercising judgement, contributing to debate about policy, being aware both of societal problems and of the difficulties in finding solutions to them. Such a view of participation, normative as it is, relates to a perspective on government, policy-making, and service provision seen from the viewpoint of individual citizens: the perspective of the mass rather than of the élite. It is, however, not the only mass perspective which might be adopted: at least three others could be suggested.

First, participation in service provision can be seen as a means by which individuals may protect their rights as consumers of public goods and services. Just as the consumer has rights which protect his interest in relation to services and goods provided in the market place by the private sector, it is argued that he should have his interests protected in relation to those goods and services for which there is either no market or where the State has replaced the private sector as provider. In other words, the public should be protected as consumers of public goods, and participation in decisions about the nature and delivery of such goods is one way to do this. We will develop this point more fully later on as this consumer perspective seems to be acquiring support among élite decision-makers by comparison with some of the more extensive perspectives.

A second mass perspective on participation might best be described as the right to consultation. From the point of view of the individual citizen, it is important to have the opportunity to express his opinion and put his point of view to those in authority. He wants to be consulted on those matters which affect him, particularly those which do so directly and in the immediate future. Proposals for new roads, reorganisation of schools and the closure of hospitals are examples of occasions when those affected will not only want to express their views but will expect to be able to do so. Much of the development of participation in planning, housing and transportation has been of this kind, though it is perhaps less well developed in such services as education, social services, and health. In many respects, old-fashioned planning inquiries (most notably the 'big' public inquiries associated with Windscale, the Vale of Belvoir or the third London Airport) and the newer examinations in public of structure plans, enshrine this principle: objectors have the right to be heard. The main change involved in more recent planning participation has been to consult people before proposals are finalised rather than after they have been formulated. The potential impact of those consulted is obviously enhanced by such earlier involvement.

A third individual perspective on participation involves the idea of people sharing in the processes of policy-making and service provision so that they may determine or share in the determination of policy and service content. This is a perspective adopted by many radical advocates of participation who believe that people have the right to decide for themselves the factors which shape their own destinies and life chances, and that, *pace* Aristotle or Rousseau, local issues and problems can be resolved by all local inhabitants coming together to settle their differences. Such a view of participation involves some transfer of power from existing élites or policy-makers to the wider community, as well as involving much wider and more frequent interaction among those concerned. In earlier work we used the idea of interactive participation to describe this kind of participation, concluding that there was little experience of it in the field of structure planning. Our present review of other services suggests a similar conclusion.

Interactive participation does find support, however, in the arguments concerning community participation discussed in Chapter 3. In that setting, it appears to counter the power of the professionals and established élites, but the scale on which it can be achieved is obviously small. Local communities and neighbourhoods, or 'home areas', offer the best chance of success, but only relate directly to service policy in such matters as the General Improvement Area or Housing Action Area, or in relation to small facilities such as primary schools or community centres. Even where such favourable conditions apply, this form of participation has not avoided radical criticism. On the one hand it has been argued that community participation operates at the wrong level. The cause of local problems is seen to lie at higher levels (national and sometimes international) and solutions must be sought at those levels. On the other hand there is a more general criticism of this and other forms of participation, that they involve nothing more than incorporation into the local power structure and offer merely token opportunity. The division of opinion about such participation has tended to inhibit its wider development.

So far we have considered three perspectives on participation from the point of view of those who receive policies and services and suggested why ordinary individuals might want to be involved. There are equally important perspectives on participation from the point of view of those who make decisions and provide services. The perspectives of this group, the élite, may well differ from those of individual citizens.

The first of these élite perspectives stresses the value of participation as a legitimating device, securing support for those in authority and for the taking of particular decisions about policy and service. Much of the participation in relation to structure plans is of this kind: publicity campaigns for proposals, public meetings, surveys and the like. These leave the public feeling it has been involved, but largely leave the decision-makers to do as they like. Other examples can be found in housing and transportation and we would conclude that this mode of participation is most heavily favoured by those in authority locally. It involves minimal action; secures support for their proposals; and for very little effort enjoys high symbolic value. The authority is able to point to a range of visible activities and often to quantifiable involvement without real threat to the prevailing distribution of power.

Groups and individuals drawn into this mode of participation often find themselves subject to the criticism levelled at community participation. Many of the methods used in legitimating participation lend themselves to the charge that groups have been co-opted or become incorporated. The problem for groups in the community is that failure to respond to opportunities of this kind makes it difficult for them to exert any influence at all. Often the same techniques serve different participatory ends, and it is the conflict of intention between decision-makers and participants which is problematic. Channels of influence viewed from below are often no more than channels of support when viewed from above.

The second élite perspective points to the utility of participation as a way of improving policies and services. This instrumental view of participation is frequently used by professional officers involved in policy-making and service provision to justify quite elaborate exercises in participation. Information collection describes this form of participation which is usually practised through sample surveys, public meetings, consultative committees and the like. Clearly these methods provide information often not available in any other way and from sources which do not usually contribute to decision-making. If officers can digest and use it, such information may well improve decisions. What it may also do, given the organisation of much participation in the public sector, is enhance the power of professional officers in relation to their elected 'masters'. Councillors often counter such officer attempts to use information in this way by pointing to their own extensive sources of such information. Their daily contact with the public, their frequent surgeries for constituents, their exposure to the views of party members, and their involvement in some participatory exercises, allow councillors to argue from their own well-informed base. Whatever the outcome of the dialogue between officers and members, and our review suggests they are usually in agreement, both the use of information and the decision-making remain in their hands. This is not a perspective which gives the public power, though its views may in some cases have some influence.

There is no third perspective from the élite point of view to match the mass perspective which favours a shift of power. Elites do not favour such transfers. They are concerned to improve their capacity through the acquisition of more information and to reinforce their decisive positions through popular support. They are not about to give power to the people. In this regard they enjoy powerful control over the means of access to decisions about public services and can often screen out contributions after they have been made. Of course, the decision-makers do not eliminate all external views. Rather they operate selectively so that only a limited range of views are heard. This practice raises important questions about the bias inherent in the choices which decision-makers make about who will be heard. This apparent bias is a vital issue to which we will return after consideration of the various services and the way in which their character affects participation.

The varied perspectives on participation adopted by both élites and general public have to be seen in relation to the diverse characteristics of the different services. Fulfilment of any of the aims just discussed must depend on the ease or difficulty of securing participation and the particular perspectives of each professional group and their clientele. Even in relation to conventional political participation through the normal processes of local government the services vary widely. Health, as we have seen, is organised separately, and its nominated structure protects its formal institutions from easy political access. For the other services elected local government should make such access easier, and yet there are wide variations between these services, often reflecting their particular origins. Education has self-contained politics which are somewhat removed from the rest of council work. For the first thirty years it was organised through separate school boards and these created distinct patterns, reinforced by the scale of the service, which have continued within the subsequent local education authorities. Other services are less marked in this respect though each reflects the fragmentary history of local government and the tendency to create new departments and committees when new services are undertaken. Recent attempts at corporate management and planning have aimed at reducing that fragmentation, as did Seebohm for the social services, but processes and actions have not yet matched intentions. Organisational fragmentation remains common, and lends itself to quite different approaches to participation by different departments.

The characteristics of each department are given a chance to bear on participation by virtue of departmental separation. One such characteristic is the target population for the service being offered, and the degree to which it operates universally or selectively. Planning, as we have seen, operates a system of control over both activity and objection to proposed activity which maintains planning as highly universal in scope. Precautions are taken to notify everyone in an area of any planned proposals and at the wider structure plan level it is understood that the whole population may be affected by what is proposed. The traditional concern among planners to protect 'the public interest' reflects this universalism, though the assumption of a single public interest looks rather naive. Despite that, the universality of planning should enhance participation, though it does not seem to do so in practice on any large scale. This may reflect the low salience of many planning issues for people, or the fact that the form and timing of planning activity distance people from the direct implications of plans.

This position is reversed in the case of housing and education both of which are less universal in their impact than planning, but which affect those who are involved much more directly and immediately. One would expect this intensity to lend itself to greater participation and this is true in the first sense of participation raised in this chapter. Parents of school children and tenants of council houses participate, but usually to seek consumer satisfaction or protection. Particular individual problems are raised and particular individual solutions are sought. This reflects the character of these services which both produce individual goods – school places and council houses. Recent policy developments have begun to change that feature, however, and some decisions have become more akin to those taken in planning. Our earlier chapters suggest some consequent increase in participation either in the sense of consultation, or in some cases seeking a transfer of power.

Areal policies have emerged in both services through the creation of Housing Action Areas and Educational Priority Areas, and these have enhanced the collective aspects of each service. The holistic approach to housing improvement in an area, to include environmental as well as direct housing action, produces collective effects and possible collective involvement. The same is true for schools when the community basis of a school is recognised and the interdependence of school and local community asserted and desired. More recently this collective aspect of education has been reinforced by the need for schools to be reorganised or to be closed. This was recognised in the 1944 Education Act with its requirement that closures or substantial changes in a school must be publicly announced in order to allow parental objection to be made to the Secretary of State. Collective issues of this kind cannot be met by the traditional consumerist tactics and require more collective

efforts. In both services there are signs of steps being taken to insti-
tutionalise such collective participation, through tenants' associations, parents' associations, and parent representation on school
governing bodies. Early evidence, as we have seen, confirms the
development but not a successful impact for such bodies.

In neither case is it easy to secure collective action in geographical localities. School catchment areas are seldom watertight and not
everyone within them has children in school. Even small housing
areas are often marked by diversity of tenure and consequent dependence on public sector housing policy. In other services this
locational feature is just not present. For example, in transport the
many users share little common geographical focus, except on a
highly localised base. The campaigns for improved services reflect
this: they are either about detailed local concerns, or about commu-
ters as a general category. This characteristic is reinforced by the
market nature of transport services which emphasise the consumer
aspects of the service.

The personal social services represent an even more extreme
position. They are very selective, catering for only a small part of
the population. In addition, they still offer very individualised services in spite of the development of residential care and of community work. This produces the expected corollary of low public
participation and a strong tendency for any involvement to manifest itself in individual pressure for consumer benefit. Individuals
get improved service, but successful cases rarely create any wider
policy impact beneficial to other clients. In aggregate such cases
may have an influence, but social service departments are not organised to reap the collective benefits involved. Quite the contrary.
Much of their working style promotes the idea that the individual
is central. For the individuals concerned, collective changes would
limit their relative advantage over fellow clients without consumer
skills.

The twin aspects of differential selectivity and differential degree
of intensity of concern with services go a long way towards explaining levels of participation. But the character of the clientele is as
important as its scale or its universality. Where there is genuine
universality, then obviously the whole social spectrum is involved,
but as we have seen, in terms of participation it is the middle-class
segment which gets involved. In other words, universality of service does not secure universality of participation. The same division is present in other, more segmental services. Generally speaking participation is dependent on the motivation and competence of

the populations served. Education serves the whole social spectrum with consequent variation in patterns of both consumerism and participation. The localisation of schools, and the creation of neighbourhood catchments with comprehensive reorganisation, have reinforced this tendency. The housing markets guarantee a degree of local, social and economic homogeneity; middle-class neighbourhoods are more likely to participate in educational matters than are working class areas.

Housing is different. The public sector does not cater for a homogeneous public; but there is a broad tendency for it to be restricted to the lower income sections of the social spectrum. Tenant participation reflects that fact. Socially heterogeneous Housing Action Areas could change the position, though tenure differences would tend to suggest heavy collective concentration on environmental rather than on purely housing issues. Personal social services represent an even more acute picture. Their clientele is not only small in number, it is by definition drawn from the least privileged and least participant section of society. They may learn consumer skills by experience, but the capacity for collective participation does not automatically follow. Community work might offer possibilities, primarily by associating clients with other nonclient local residents.

Despite their obvious importance, the nature of each service and of its clientele are not the only determinants of the level of participation. It is as much a function of the staff and organisation in each of the different services. We have noted two prevailing modes of organisation relevant to different kinds of staff. These modes affect staff activity and attitudes in different ways and, in turn, influence the way in which the public and the clientele are regarded. Most obvious, given the character of most local government services, is the degree of professionalism present. Most services exhibit some professional features, though the more personal and less clear-cut areas show less clarity in this respect. Health is the obvious primary example of the highly professionalised service, but planning displays similar characteristics. Education falls somewhat short of that degree of professionalism, while personal social services and housing management occupy the weakest position in this regard. Even in these latter two cases, however, there is a marked tendency to seek the form and status enjoyed by the more professionalised services. In that respect they are most interesting in relation to participation. As we have seen, their clientele are among those least able to participate, at least in current terms. This is offset to some extent by the overt commitment by the professionals to participation by the clientele. At the same time, the search for professional status tends to require that staff operate with a high degree of autonomy, conditioned by the control of their peers and not of their clients. The resultant tension is obvious. If the corollary of social work or housing management becoming professionalised is the adoption of norms derived from medicine, then our earlier discussion of participation in these various fields suggests tensions for the groups concerned.

In neither case is such professional development certain. Both show many of the hallmarks of the alternative, bureaucratic, form of organisation. Close supervision is prescribed for the field-worker in both housing and social services, denying the autonomy which is usual in professional practice. Such supervision is sometimes justified in terms of the uncertainties inherent in these softer areas of work, but it also derives from managerial needs in relation to various aspects of the service. The former is relevant to the issues of consumer participation, while the latter poses problems for wider participation as we saw in the case of community work in social services. Not that the bureaucratic mode is favourable to participation. It is more a case of a different basis from which to explain (and sometimes to justify) non-participation, and results in different problems for those seeking to encourage such participation. The formality and institutionalisation of bureaucracy make for inflexibility which militates against participation of all kinds. At the consumer level, there is less slack available for the client to manipulate. At the more collective level, the inertia in such systems makes them highly resistant to change and therefore to participation. Participation may not mean change, but it carries an inherent risk that change is what will be demanded.

These variations between services are important to the form and shape of any participation which takes place, but as we have shown, they do not make for much ultimate difference in the actual degree of participation offered. There is no service where participation is very high, even in cases where legislation requires it. Both professionalism and bureaucracy are resistant to outside participation and to client consumerism. Each requires that power remain with insiders, acting either according to established and acknowledged professional norms, or to bureaucratic rules sanctioned by political approval. Neither model allows a large role for the public, except perhaps through the conventional political processes; and the professional structure even raises doubts about that approach.

Participation is weak, while consumerism rests on client acquisition of knowledge of professional rules and bureaucratic systems. Both are rare; and while the emergence of client advocacy may produce consumer success in some cases, it does not change the overall position of client weakness.

When one combines these elements of scope and type of clientele with service character and type of staffing, a clear pattern is discernible. Congruence between departmental style and client incapacity, as in transport and health care, produces very low participation. Dominant staff in both services opt for the élite model of participation as a manner of legitimising their decisions, while in transport the market is seen to take care of consumer interests. In the case of health care, the incidence of illness produces only periodic need for participation and high incapacity at the points where it is most necessary. In transport, a widely dispersed constituency is hard to mobilise unless, as with London commuting, there is very high density of use of public transport and limited alternative possibilities in the market.

There are no examples of highly participatory services so the opposite polar model is not present. Our analysis suggests that there is no possibility of such a model developing in practice, despite much current lip service to participation. Elite domination of public services is universal and, as we have said, élite attitudes tend to favour models of participation which strictly limit the role of the public. At the same time, few services have clientele drawn exclusively from the middle class who might press for greater opportunities for participation, except in so far as services can be focused precisely in geographical terms. Where that is the case, such middle-class localities can often achieve their aims at the expense of other, working-class, localities. There is seldom a common interest to bind both groups and consequently little pressure from below claiming any transfer of power.

If participation is affected by the nature of the different services, it is also affected by the way in which policy for the various services is determined largely at the centre rather than in the locality. Here we return to the process of central–local government relations and to the national world of policy-making, particularly that part of it which is dominated by the national institutions of local government and by the central departments with overall responsibility for these services.

Much of the discussion concerning policy initiatives and the broad statements of policy that are contained in legislation, as well as that concerning the guidelines for policy implementation and service standards, takes place on the national rather than the local stage. It is a stage on which the main actors are the national pressure groups concerned with services, the national associations of local authorities, and the relevant professional bodies, who meet with Ministers, possibly with Members of Parliament, and overwhelmingly with civil servants.

The drama which these actors play out can determine the future of each service, though it is often more symbolic in character, having limited direct impact, but satisfying the public and thus legitimising the actions of central government. Interest groups can be seen to be serving their members' interests, lobbying Parliament and conferring with Ministers, and winning enough concessions to sustain this mode of action. Members of Parliament are seen to be looking after constituents and Ministers are seen to be active.

Behind this public activity much more is taking place, sometimes being glimpsed on the stage itself. It is backstage, or in the wings, that the local government and professional associations negotiate with civil servants about the realities of politics and the possibilities for policy. In recent years these established bodies have been joined by trade union representatives from the National Union of Public Employees (NUPE) and the National and Local Government Officers (NALGO) and the character of their muscle has given the debate more publicity. Unlike their professional counterparts, the unions are forced to resort to sanctions like strikes and sit-ins, which have protected jobs and service standards as well as disturbing the traditional covert system of decision-making.

The Local Government and Planning Act of 1980 provides an excellent example of this form of active involvement, while discussions are likely to be less extensive and less vigorous over issues such as the annual grant settlement, the introduction of new circulars by central government, or the relaxation of planning controls. As at the local level, a few major decisions engage a wide range of people, but once they are decided there is much less active involvement. In addition, even where it does take place, the participation is of an exclusive kind. Essentially it is consultation by the centre of those whose active support is necessary if new policies are to work, or savings be made. Central government has the formal power to change the policies of both local government and the health service, but is only likely to do so after consultation. The same is true for other aspects of government policy. Our two- or three-tier system of government means that the centre has to carry the localities with it in relation to policy development, which helps to explain the gradualism and caution inherent in many areas of policy.

Whilst this national stage provides an opportunity for many people who are prominent local leaders to play a part in national policy-making, obtaining a part is not easy. National discussions about policy and service delivery are very closed: those seeking access to them, be they individuals or groups, have to establish not only their *right* to be consulted, but also their reliability, trustworthiness and utility. Selective and selected participation is the most appropriate phrase to describe this process which sets the broad parameters within which local services and policies are subsequently determined. It is a process different in some respects from the type of participation with which we have been concerned. It excludes not only individuals from the discussion, but also most localities. Individual local authorities or health authorities are unlikely to be involved with central government over broad policy matters. For them, it is the specific, local issue, which is likely to promote contact: a sort of authority level consumerism. Hospital closures, or the route of a particular road, are the kinds of issue which individual authorities (and individuals within them) will seek to raise. The centre may find it difficult to respond, partly because it wants to deal in generalities and to treat all localities (in theory at least) equally, and partly because it experiences difficulties in penetrating the barriers raised by the various national policy networks, of which the one for local government is but one example. This means that participation in these critical discussions at national level is exclusive and involves a bias against particular localities who do not find representation. Recent attempts to generate local participation, even when stimulated from the centre, have done nothing to open up the central processes to wider participation.

The result is severe limitations being placed on local governments in their consideration of policy. National parameters limit local opportunity and are reinforced by the fact that local participation displays many of the same features just discussed in a national setting. In many ways there is another bias operating at the local level, one which reflects the accessibility of both local government and health authorities to those who possess the necessary combination of participatory skills, knowledge and motivation. In essence it is a bias (though not an exclusive one) in favour of the middle class and the major local élites – of the well organised and the competent. These are the participants who understand the rules of the game, even if they are not necessarily able to determine them. Usually those rules have been made by people who share the same background as these local élites. The national parameters and the rules of participation do not threaten middle-class interests. To participate within them is satisfactory from their point of view. Other local interests are doubly disadvantaged by this. National policy limits and the local rules of the game invariably militate against them, leaving them with little more than recourse to consumerism.

That the middle class participate more frequently in the issues involved in local service provision has been repeatedly demonstrated throughout this book. In planning, transportation, the health service, and education, we find that it is middle-class individuals and middle-class organisations who become involved on the majority of occasions. Even in those services where benefits are more likely to go to working-class recipients, such as social services and housing, the individualistic client approach of the professionals involved, and the mode of service delivery, inhibits a class-based participation, as the difficulties of claimants' unions and tenants' associations amply demonstrate. Indeed, even those groups who comprise the recognised voluntary sector in social service provision, such as the WRVS, tend to be dominated by middle-class members.

In other words, though there have been great moves towards public involvement in local service provision in recent years, little has been achieved by way of a fundamental shift in power, a shift which implicitly underlay the ideas of radical proponents of participation in the late 1960s. In the end, élite perspectives have won out, and participation has served the purposes of building up a consensus for the proposals of those in power, thereby legitimating them. As such, public participation over the last ten years has performed an important symbolic function in British local and national politics but with a few small-scale exceptions, it has failed to achieve all that its proponents wished.

REFERENCES

ABRAMS, P. (1977) Community care: some research problems and priorities, *Policy and Politics*, **6**, 125–51.

ALDOUS, T. (1980) Questions of 'Sax', *Municipal J.*, 257–8.

ALEXANDER REPORT (1975) *Challenge of Change*, Scottish Education Department, Edinburgh.

ANDREWS, C.L. (1979) *Tenants and Town Hall*, HMSO, London.

ARMYTAGE, W.H.G. (1965) *Four Hundred Years of English Education*, Cambridge University Press, Cambridge.

BACON, W. (1978) *Public Accountability and the Schooling System*, Harper and Row, London.

BAINS REPORT (1972) *The New Local Authorities: Management and Structure*, HMSO, London.

BARNARD, K. AND LEE, K. (1977) *Conflicts in the National Health Service*, Croom Helm, London.

BOADEN, N. AND COLLINS, N. (1975) *Group Consultation in Merseyside Structure Planning*, Linked Research Project into Public Participation in Structure Planning, Interim Research Paper 6, Sheffield.

BOADEN, N., GOLDSMITH, M., HAMPTON, W. AND STRINGER, P. (1980) *Planning and Participation in Practice: a study of public participation in structure planning*, Pergamon, Oxford.

BOADEN, N. AND WALKER, R. (1976) *Sample Surveys and Public Participation*, Linked Research Project into Public Participation in Structure Planning, Interim Research Paper 10, Sheffield.

BOCHEL, DOROTHY AND MACLARAN, MORAG (1979) Representing the interests of the public? The case of the Local Health Council in Scotland, *Journal of Social Policy*, **8**, 449–72.

BRAMLEY, G., LEATNER, P. AND MURIE, A. (1979) *Housing Strategies and Investment Programmes*, Working Paper 7, School for Advanced Urban Studies, University of Bristol.

BRITISH ASSOCIATION OF SOCIAL WORKERS (1977) *A Code of Ethics for Social Work*, Birmingham.

BUCHANAN REPORT (1963) *Traffic in Towns*, HMSO, London.

BULLOCK REPORT (1975) *A Language for Life*, HMSO, London.

BULLOCK REPORT (1977) *Report of the Committee of Inquiry on Industrial Democracy*, HMSO, London.

BURBIDGE, M. (1975) Learning from our mistakes, *Municipal J., Housing Management Supplement*, 31 October, 13–15.

CAMPBELL, H. (1976) 'Suddenly, everyone . . .', *Voluntary Housing*, **8**, 15–16.

CASTELLS, M. (1975) *The Urban Question*, Edward Arnold, London; and (1979) *City, Class and Power*, Macmillan, London.

CENTRAL HOUSING ADVISORY COMMITTEE (1938) *The Management of Municipal Housing Estates*, HMSO, London.

CHARTERED INSTITUTE OF PUBLIC FINANCE (1976) *Transport Policies and Programmes: the new planning approach*, London.

COCKBURN, CYNTHIA (1977) *The Local State*, Pluto Press, London.

COMMUNITY DEVELOPMENT PROJECT (1974) *Inter. Project Report*, National Community Development Project, London.

CORDEN, J. (1980) Contract in Social Work Practice, *British Journal of Social Work*, **10**, 143–62.

COUGER, M. AND DAVIS, R. (1977) An alternative to the public inquiry, *The Planner*, May, 16–18.

CULLINGWORTH, J.B. (1972) *Town and Country Planning in Britain*, Allen and Unwin, London.

DAVIES, J.G. (1972) *The Evangelistic Bureaucrat: a study of a planning exercise in Newcastle upon Tyne*, Tavistock, London.

DENNIS, N. (1970) *People and Planning: the sociology of housing in Sunderland*, Faber and Faber, London.

DENNIS, N. (1972) *Public Participation and Planners' Blight*, Faber and Faber, London.

DEPARTMENT OF THE ENVIRONMENT (1967) *Town and Country Planning*, HMSO, London.

DEPARTMENT OF THE ENVIRONMENT (1973a) *Publicity for Planning Applications, Appeals and Other Proposals for Development*, Circular 71/73, HMSO, London.

DEPARTMENT OF THE ENVIRONMENT (1973b) *Public Participation in General Improvement Areas*, Area Improvement Note 8, HMSO, London.

DEPARTMENT OF THE ENVIRONMENT (1973c) *Structure Plans: the examination in public*, HMSO, London.

DEPARTMENT OF THE ENVIRONMENT (1975a) *Housing Act 1974: Parts IV, V, VI. Housing Action Areas, Priority Neighbourhoods and General Improvement Areas*, DOE Circular 14/75, HMSO, London.

DEPARTMENT OF THE ENVIRONMENT (1975b) *Final Report of the Working Party on Housing Co-operatives*, HMSO, London.

DEPARTMENT OF THE ENVIRONMENT (1977) *Housing Strategies and Investment Programmes: arrangements for 1978/79*, Circular 63/77, HMSO, London.

DEPARTMENT OF THE ENVIRONMENT, (1978a) *Report of a Study of General Improvement Areas 1969–76*, Circular 63/78, HMSO, London.

DEPARTMENT OF THE ENVIRONMENT (1978b) *Housing Strategies and Investment Programmes for Local Authorities in England: arrangements for 1979/80*, Circular 38/78, HMSO, London.

DEPARTMENT OF TRANSPORT (1977) *Transport Policy*, HMSO, London.

DEPARTMENT OF TRANSPORT (1978a) *Report on the Review of Highway Inquiry Procedures*, HMSO, London.

DEPARTMENT OF TRANSPORT (1978b) *Report of the Advisory Committee on Trunk Road Assessment*, HMSO, London.

DEPARTMENT OF TRANSPORT (1978c) *Transport Act 1978, Public Transport Planning in non-Metropolitan Counties*, Circular 8/78, HMSO, London.

DEPARTMENT OF TRANSPORT (1978d) *A Guide to Community Transport*, HMSO, London.

DEPARTMENT OF TRANSPORT (1980) *Policy for Roads: England*, HMSO, London.

DOBRY, G. (1975) *Review of the Development Control System*, HMSO, London.

Education Act, 1944, HMSO, London.

EVANS, W. (1978) Public Inquiries and disruptions, *New Law Journal*, 23 March, 291–3.

FERRIS, J. (1972) *Participation in Urban Planning: the Barnsbury Case*, G. Bell and Sons, London.

FRANCKLOW, R. (1979) Getting it right for the tenant, *Housing*, July, 6–7.

GOLDSTEIN, H. (1973) *Social Work Practice: unitary approach*, University of South Carolina Press, Columbia, South Carolina.

GRANT, J. (1977) *The Politics of Urban Transport Planning*, Earth Resources Research, London.

GREGORY, R. (1971) *The Price of Amenity*, Macmillan, London.

HALL, A.S. (1974) *The Point of Entry*, Allen and Unwin, London.

HALSEY, A.H. (ed.) (1972) *Educational Priority*, HMSO, London.

HAMER, M. (1974) *Wheels within Wheels; a study of the road lobby*, Friends of the Earth, London.

HAMPTON, W. (1970) *Democracy and Community*, Oxford University Press, London.

HAMPTON, W. (1979) Adult education and the urban programme, *Town and Country Planning*, **48**, 152–6.

HAMPTON, W. (1980) Adult education for participation, *Studies in Adult Education*, **12**, 117–26.

HART, D.A. (1976) *Strategic Planning in London: the rise and fall of the primary road network*, Pergamon, Oxford.

HAYES, J. (1963) Tenants' associations, *Society of Housing Managers' Quarterly*, July, 7–9.

HIRSCHMAN, A.O. (1970) *Exit, Voice and Loyalty*, Harvard University Press, Cambridge, Mass.

HORN, C.J. *et al.* (1977) *Area Management: objectives and structures*, Institute of Local Government Studies, University of Birmingham.

Housing Review (1975) September–October, 134.

HUMBLE, S. AND TALBOT, J. (1977) *Neighbourhood Councils in England: a report to the Department of the Environment*, Institute of Local Government Studies, Birmingham. cf. Talbot and Humble, op. cit.

JAQUES, E, (1978) *Health Services*, Heinemann, London.

Journal of the Town Planning Institute (1968) July–August.

KIMBER. R. AND RICHARDSON, J.J. (eds) (1974) *Campaigning for the Environment*, Routledge and Kegan Paul, London.

KLEIN, R. AND LEWIS, JANET (1976) *The Politics of Consumer Representation*, Centre for Studies in Social Policy, London.

KOGAN, M. (1974) *Educational Policy Making*, Allen and Unwin, London.

LAYFIELD REPORT, (1976) *Report of the Committee of Inquiry into Local Government Finance*, HMSO, London.

LEE, M. (1963) *Social Leaders and Public Persons*, Oxford University Press, London.

LEVITT, RUTH (1976) *The Reorganised National Health Service*, Croom Helm, London.

Local Government and Planning Act (1980) HMSO, London.

LOWE, S. (1977) Community groups and local politics, in Darke, R. and Walker, R. (eds) *Local Government and the Public*, Leonard Hill, London.

MCKEAN, J.M. (1976) D-o-it-yourself, *Building Design*, 30 April, 14–15.

MACKENZIE, W.J.M. (1979) *Power and Responsibility in Health Care: the NHS as a political institution*, Nuffield Provincial Hospitals Trust and Oxford University Press, London.

MALPASS, P. (1976) The politics of participation, *Architects J.*, **169**, 1011–21.

MASTERSON, M. (1978) Community councils, *Scottish Legal Action Group Bulletin*; and (1979) The creation of Scotland's national system of official voluntarism, *Journal of Voluntary Action Research*, **8**, Parts 3–4.

MAYER, J.E. AND TIMMS, N. (1970) *The Client Speaks*, Routledge and Kegan Paul, London.

MOWAT, C.L. (1961) *The Charity Organisation Society 1869–1913*, Methuen, London.

MYNORS, P.L.B. AND MOORE, M.D. (1978) Public involvement in road planning: the Leicester experiment, *The Highway Engineer*, **25**, 2–5/17.

NATIONAL CONSUMER COUNCIL (1978) *Rural Rides: experiments in rural public transport–a consumer view*, London.

National Health Service Reorganisation Act (1973) HMSO, London.

PARIS, C. AND BLACKABY, B. (1979) *Not Much Improvement: urban renewal policy in Birmingham*, Heinemann, London.

PETERS R.S. (ed.) (1969) *Perspectives on Plowden*, Routledge and Kegan Paul, London.

PLANNING ADVISORY GROUP (1965) *The Future of Development Plans*, HMSO, London.

PLOWDEN REPORT (1967) *Children and their Primary Schools*, HMSO, London.

PULLEN, D. (1978) *Community Work in Practice 2: The Neighbourhood Projects Group*, Course DE 206, Open University, Milton Keynes.

REGAN, D.E. (1977) *Local Government and Education*, Allen and Unwin, London.

RAWP (1976) *Sharing Resources for Health in England: Report of the Resource Allocation Working Party*, HMSO, London.

RICHARDSON, A. AND KENDALL, B. (1975) The progress of participation, *Housing Monthly*, September, 20–24.

ROBINSON, D. AND HENRY, S. (1977) *Self-Help and Health: mutual aid for modern problems*, Martin Robertson, Oxford.

Royal Commission on Local Government in England: Report (1969) Vols 1 and 2, HMSO, London.

Royal Commission on Local Government in England, Research Study 9, *Community Attitudes Survey: England* (1969) HMSO, London.

Royal Commission on the National Health Service: Report (1979) HMSO, London.

RUSSELL REPORT (1973) *Adult Education: a plan for development*, HMSO, London.

SAUNDERS, P. (1979) *Urban Politics*, Hutchinson, London.

SEEBOHM REPORT (1968) *Report of the Committee on Local Authority and Allied Personal Services*, HMSO, London.

SHARMAN, F.A. (1977) John Tyme and highway inquiries: an interim report, *J. of Planning and Environmental Law*, 293–8.

SHARPE, L.J. (1970) Theories of local government, *Political Studies*, **18**, 153–74.

SIMPSON, H.G. (1976) Tenant participation in housing, *Housing Monthly*, October, 12–14.

SKEFFINGTON REPORT (1969) *People and Planning*, HMSO, London.

SOCIAL AND COMMUNITY PLANNING AND RESEARCH (1975) personal communication.

SOLACE/INLOGOV, *The Local Government Bill No. 2: An Appraisal*, Society of Local Government Chief Executives/Institute of Local Government Studies, Birmingham.

STACEY, F. (1978) *Ombudsmen Compared*, Oxford University Press, London.

STRINGER, P. (1978) *Tuning in to the Public: survey before participation*, Interim Research Paper 14, Linked Research Project into Public Participation in Structure Planning, Sheffield.

STRINGER, P. (1981) A comparison of the parish councils and voluntary groups in action, *J. of Voluntary Action Research*, in press.

TALBOT, J. AND HUMBLE, S. (1976) *A Survey of Neighbourhood Groups in England*, Institute of Local Government Studies, Birmingham. cf. Humble and Talbot, op. cit.

TAYLOR REPORT (1977) *A New Partnership for our Schools*, HMSO, London.

THORNLEY, M. (1977) Tenement rehabilitation in Glasgow, in Darke, R. and Walker, R. (eds) *Local Government and the Public*, Leonard Hill, London.

THORNTON, P. AND STRINGER, P. (1979) The role of local groups in trunk road construction; a case study, *J. of Voluntary Action Research*, **8**, 84–93.

The Times, 27 May 1980.

Town and Country Planning Act (1968) HMSO, London.

TOWNSEND, P. (1962) *The Last Refuge*, Routledge and Kegan Paul, London.

TYME, J. (1975) M-way inquiries: a corruption of government? *New Scientist*, 6 November, 320–2.

TYME, J. (1978) *Motorways versus Democracy*, Macmillan, London.

WARDROPER, J. (1978) Road men in reverse? *The Sunday Times*, 12 February.

WATKIN, B. (1978) *The National Health Service: the first phase 1948–1974 and after*, Allen and Unwin, London.

WINFIELD, R. (1979) Public transport plans: an effective planning discipline, *Surveyor*, **154**, 26–8.

YOUNG, K. (1975) *Local Politics and the Rise of Party*, Leicester University Press, Leicester.

Note: The Interim Research Papers, Linked Research Project into Public Participation in Structure Planning, can be obtained only from Department of the Environment, DPRP2, Becket House, 1, Lambeth Palace Road, London, SE1 7ER.

INDEX

Abrams, P., 133
action groups *see* pressure groups
Adult Education: a plan for development,
  see Russell Report
Age Concern, 24, 127
Aldous, T., 74
Amenity Groups, 76–7
Andrews, C.L., 103
Area Management schemes, 43
Armytage, W.H.G., 151
ASSIST team (Glasgow), 109–10
Association of London Housing Estates,
  100
Assn. of Neighbourhood Councils, 47,
  48, 49

Bacon, W., 160–1
Bains Report: *The New Local
  Authorities: Management and
  Structure*, 120
Barnard, K. & Lee, K., 126
Boaden, N. & Collins, N., 122
Boaden, N., Goldsmith, M., Hampton,
  W. & Stringer, P., 65, 87, 123, 167
Boaden, N., & Walker, R., 124–5
Bochel, D. & Maclaran, M., 121–2
Bramley, G., Leatner, P., & Murie, A.,
  100
British Assn. of Social Workers, 25,
  133–4
  Code of Ethics for Social Work,
    136–7
Buchanan, Sir Colin, 59
Buchanan Report: *Traffic in Towns*, 75
Bullock Report (1975): *A Language for
  Life*, 160, 162

Bullock Report (1977): *Report of the
  Committee of Inquiry on Industrial
  Democracy*, 164
Burbidge, M., 109

Campbell, H., 106
Castells, M., 33
CBI, 24
Central Housing Advisory Committee
  (CHAC): *The Management of
  Municipal Housing Estates*, 111
central-local government relations, 5,
  6–8, 56, 176–9
  control of finance, 18, 20–2, 30,
    72–3, 93
  involvement with local schemes,
    42–6, 79–80, 97–8, 106–7,
    140
  issues to be resolved at both levels,
    17–24
Chartered Institute of Public Finance,
  (CIPF): *Transport Policies and
  Programmes: the new planning
  approach*, 73
Child Poverty Action Group (CPAG),
  24, 119–20, 127
Children and their Primary Schools see
  Plowden Report
Children's Panels (Scotland), 165
Cockburn, C., 44
Community Attitudes Survey: England
  (commissioned by Royal
  Commission on Local Government
  in England), 36–7
Community Attitudes Survey on
  Scotland (commissioned by Royal

187

Public participation in local services

Housing Corporation
  backed co-operative housing, 108, 152
  encourages tenants' involvement in managing housing associations, 41
  involvement with inner city rehabilitation and special need housing, 108
  parallels with integration of public and private provision in education, 152
  in Scotland, 110
  taken over management functions local authority might have exercised, 93–4
Housing Strategies and Investment Programmes (HIPs), 99–100
Housing Strategies and Investment Programmes: arrangements for 1978/9 see DOE
Housing Strategies and Investment Programmes for Local Authorities in England: arrangements for 1979/80 see DOE

Inner Area Studies (Birmingham, Liverpool and Southwark), 43
Institute of Housing, 94–5
Institute of Local Govt. Studies (INLOGOV), 43
interest groups *see* pressure groups

Kimber, R. & Richardson, J.J., 76
Klein, R., & Lewis, J., 125
Kogan, M., 157

Labour Governments
  1964–70, 23, 31
  1974–9, 24, 31, 45, 48, 155
Labour Party, 48, 104, 120
(A) Language for Life see Bullock Report (1975)
Layfield Rept., *Rept. of the Cttee of Inquiry into Local Government Finance*, 7, 22
Lee, M., 8
Leitch Committee *see* Dept. of Transport
Local Auth. Social Services Act 1970, 132

local government
  and community councils (England), 44
  and community work, 140–1
  and education, 148–9, 151–2, 153–5
  and health services, 113–15
  and housing, 90, 93–5, 99, 100–1, 105
  and housing officers, 94–5, 96–7, 97–8
  and planners and planning, 61–2
  and road planning, 74
  and social services, 131–2, 143–6
  professionalisation, 5, 6, 8–10, 19, 24–8, 174–5
  spread of parliamentary politics into, 8
  democracy & efficiency, criteria of, 2–4
  example of joint participation exercise on road planning, 74
  elected members, 10, 11, 14, 15, 16, 25–7, 29, 61, 63, 67, 96, 102, 121, 132, 140, 145, 170
  finance, 18, 21–2, 30, 33–4, 72–3
  fragmentation of, 5–6, 113, 132
  idea of locality or community, 3
  increase in scale and range, 4, 5
  increasing remoteness, 5, 11, 28–9, 34, 43
  interest in or knowledge of, 29, 37
  lack of favour for consultation paper on neighbourhood councils, 48
  national association, rise of, 8–9
  parish councils, 45, 81–2
  pragmatic nature of, in Britain, 2
  reorganisations of, 22–3, 29, 132
  responsibility for structure and local plans, 56
  stimulation of local action groups, 38
  trends, post-1945, 17
  see also central-local govt. relations
Local Government Act, 1972, 22, 45
Local Government and Planning Act, 1980
  control over local auth. spending, 18, 20, 30
  duty to inform public about its work, 31
  provokes negotiations with professional associations and